D1528211

MEDICAL SERIAL KILLERS

Sara L. Latta

Enslow Publishing

101 W. 23rd Street
Suite 240
New York, NY 10011
USA

enslow.com

Published in 2016 by Enslow Publishing, LLC.
101 W. 23rd Street, Suite 240, New York, NY 10011

Library of Congress Cataloging-in-Publication Data
Names: Latta, Sara L., author.
Title: Medical serial killers / Sara L. Latta.
Description: New York, NY : Enslow Publishing, 2016. | Series: The psychology
  of serial killers | Includes bibliographical references and index.
Identifiers: LCCN 2015030382 | ISBN 9780766072961 (library bound)
Subjects: LCSH: Serial murderers--Juvenile literature. | Medical
  personnel--Juvenile literature. | Medical ethics--Juvenile literature.
Classification: LCC HV6515 .L37 2016 | DDC 364.152/32--dc23
LC record available at http://lccn.loc.gov/2015030382

Printed in the United States of America

To Our Readers: We have done our best to make sure all websites in this book were active
and appropriate when we went to press. However, the author and the publisher have no
control over and assume no liability for the material available on those websites or on
any websites they may link to. Any comments or suggestions can be sent by e-mail to
customerservice@enslow.com.

Photo Credits: Throughout book: chrupka/Shutterstock.com (black scratched background),
Merkushev Vasiliy/Shutterstock.com (dark red background), Tiberiu Stan/Shutterstock.
com (brain waves); cover, p. 1 Benoit Daoust/Shutterstock.com (man in surgical mask); p.
7 Spotmatik Ltd/Shutterstock.com; p. 8 shironosov/iStock/Thinkstock; p. 10 Zdravinjo/
Shutterstock.com; p. 11 Leonardo da/Shutterstock.com; p. 15 Greater Manchester Police/
Getty Images News/Getty Images; pp. 17, 21 Reuters/Landov; p. 23 AP Photo/Michael Conroy;
pp. 26, 28, 31, 33, 37, 39, 46, 48, 89, 91, 113 © AP Images; p. 41 Scott Nelson/AFP/Getty
Images; p. 43 Carolyn Cole/Los Angeles Times/Getty Images; p. 53 Evening Standard/Hulton
Archive/Getty Images; p. 56 Apic/Getty Images; p. 57 Carl De Souza/AFP/Getty Images; pp.
60, 62 Chicago History Museum/Getty Images; p. 65 Courtesy of the Ohio History Connection
(State Archives 1000 AV); p. 73 © Steve Vidler/Alamy Stock Photo; p. 76 © Heritage Image
Partnership Ltd/Alamy; p. 78 © PVDE/Bridgeman Images; p. 81 Ralph Morse/The LIFE Picture
Collection/Getty Images; p. 84 © Jose Barrera/San Antonio Express-News/ZUMA Press; p. 87
ChameleonsEye/Shutterstock.com; p. 95 David Jones/PA Wire/AP Images; pp. 99, 119 Public
Domain; p. 101 Courtesy of the Cambridge Historical Society (3A.0262 CHS); p. 105 Nicole
DiMella; p. 108 Deedeebee/Wikimedia Commons/Women's Huron Valley Correctional Facility.
jpg/CC BY 3.0; p. 110 John Roca/NY Daily News Archive/Getty Images; p. 117 Linda Hazzard,
1913, Corrections Department, Penitentiary, Inmate Mug Shots, Washington State Archives;
pp. 122, 124 Fairfax Media/Getty Images; p. 127 © Sueddeutsche Zeitung Photo/Alamy; p.
129 ullstein bild/Getty Images.

Contents

The Types and Behaviors of Serial Killers

	Organized	Disorganized
IQ	105–120 (falls within normal range)	80–95 (below average)
Social skills	Normal	Poor
Childhood	Grew up with a stable father or father figure; may have encountered physical abuse	Grew up with an abusive father or no father present; may have encountered emotional abuse
Proximity of murders to home	Moves around a lot to flee murder scenes	Commits murders around home
Living situation	Married, lives with partner, or dates	Lives alone, doesn't date
Education	Possibly attended college	Dropped out of high school
Time of activity	Daytime	Nighttime
Method of ensnaring victims	Seduction	Attack
Interaction with victims	Converses with victims	Does not consider victims to be people
Method of disposal	May dismember body after killing; disposes of remains	Leaves body behind after killing; usually does not dismember
State of crime scene	Controlled; little physical evidence left behind	Chaotic; leaves physical evidence behind
Reason for returning to scene of crime	To see the police working; interest in police work	To relive the murder

Source: O'Connor, Tom. "Serial Killer Typology."
http://www.ravenndragon.net/montgomery/csi/oconnortypology1.pdf

INTRODUCTION

The vast majority of doctors, nurses, and other health care professionals have a deep and genuine desire to help people. These professionals have taken a solemn oath to heal, not harm, and we put a great deal of trust in their integrity. Yet Dr. Michael Swango, who poisoned at least four of his patients (and probably many more), wrote in his journal that he loved the "sweet, husky, close smell of indoor homicide." The murders, he wrote, were "the only way I have of reminding myself that I'm still alive."[1]

While it may be difficult to think of healers as murderers, one psychiatrist makes the case that medicine has given rise to more serial killers than all the other professions combined—with nursing coming in a close second.[2] Why? Some doctors and nurses enter the field of medicine not because they want to help people, but because they have an unhealthy fascination with life and death. Many other health care serial killers, on the other hand, stumble into the deadly habit of murder. After killing once, whether by mistake or a desire to put a suffering patient out of his misery, they find they enjoy it. In either case, it is difficult to think of a better setting for a medically trained serial killer than a hospital or nursing home. Death is not uncommon in health care facilities, and potentially deadly drugs are readily available.[3]

Serial Murders and the People Who Commit Them

The Federal Bureau of Investigation (FBI) defines serial murder as "the unlawful killing of two or more victims [often more] by the same offender(s), in separate events."[4] A serial killer always takes some emotional "time off" between murders. This sets serial killers apart from spree killers, who murder people in several different locations with no cooling-off period, and mass murderers, who kill many people at the same time in a single location.

The question of why some people become serial killers is complex. There is no generic set of conditions known to produce a serial killer. Like everyone else, the lives of serial killers are the result of biological, social, and psychological factors. That said, there are a few common developmental features that are common in many—but not all—serial killers. The first one is bed-wetting well past the age when most children stay dry throughout the night. More than sixty percent of serial killers were still wetting the bed as teenagers. The second is a fascination with fire, one that goes beyond simply playing with matches and extends to setting buildings and even other people on fire. The third red flag is a cruelty toward animals. Many kids have pulled the wings off flies or thrown firecrackers into anthills, but most soon move on to other,

Most medical professionals choose that career path to help people. Some, however, use their positions to cause more harm than good.

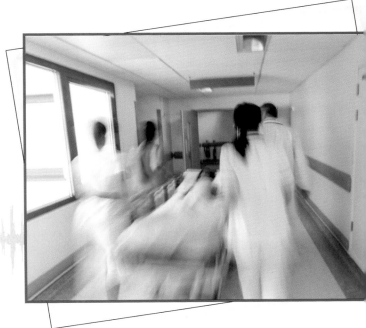

less violent pastimes. Budding serial killers, on the other hand, often take a sadistic pleasure in brutally torturing cats, dogs, and other creatures. Of course, not all children who wet the bed past adolescence, like to play with fire, or torture animals grow up to be serial killers.

Most serial killers do seem to have one thing in common: a troubled childhood. Many were the victims of abuse or neglect, or lost a parent at a critical age. Obviously, many children have terrible childhoods and do not grow up to be serial killers. But for some reason, serial killers channel the feelings of hate and self-loathing fostered during their troubled upbringing into a need to murder—again and again.

Some serial killers are mentally ill; psychotics who have lost touch with reality. Many more are psychopaths, a condition that is

Proficiency at causing destruction is one sign of psychopathic tendencies.

closely associated with antisocial personality disorder, or APD. On the surface, they appear to be perfectly normal. In fact, they may be quite charming. But underneath, they lack a sense of empathy, conscience, or guilt. They tend to blame others for their problems. They are terrific liars, they are great at manipulating others, and they have a grandiose view of themselves. Not all psychopaths are serial killers. In fact, many psychopaths are successful in politics and business. They are, after all, good at getting people to do what they want them to do.

There is no simple profile to describe a serial killer, but some experts in the field have proposed some ways of classifying these criminals. One well-known method, known as the Holmes typology (named for its creators, Ronald M. and Stephen T. Holmes), focuses on motive: What is the killer's purpose in committing the crime?

According to the Holmes typology, serial killers can be classified into four principal categories:

- **Visionary.** These killers act because they hear voices or see visions that tell them to commit murder. They generally suffer from some form of psychosis.

- **Missionary.** These killers believe they must rid society of a particular group of people they believe "bad" or "undesirable."

- **Power.** These killers are gratified by their ability to "play God" or hold the fate of another in their hands.

- **Hedonist.** These killers derive some sort of psychological or material benefit from killing. They kill because they enjoy it. This group can be further divided into three subcategories:

  - **Comfort-oriented hedonists.** These killers commit their crimes for financial or emotional personal gain.
  - **Thrill-oriented hedonists.** The act of killing gives them a rush of excitement.
  - **Lust-oriented hedonists.** These killers are sexually excited by the act of killing or their victim's dead bodies.

Visionary serial killers are rare, and there are no known examples of medical serial killers who fall into this category. This may be due to the very nature of killing in the health care setting: It very often requires careful planning and subterfuge—actions that are difficult for psychotic killers to carry out. And, while there are a few medical serial killers whose motives may have included a missionary aspect, they usually have other, overriding motives to kill—usually power or gain. The nineteenth-century physician Thomas Cream (whose profile is included in this resource), seemed

Many serial killers were abused as children, and continue the cycle of abuse into adulthood.

to target prostitutes, but the common thread throughout his killing career was greed.

There are additional categories of medical serial killers that do not fit easily into the Holmes typology. One category includes the treatment killers—often quacks—who continue to prescribe medicines or treatments long after it is clear that death is the likely outcome of their treatment. Many treatment killers are mentally ill. Many would argue that genocidal doctors who cooperate with state-run terrorism and war, including the Nazi holocaust and the Armenian genocide, should also be considered serial killers.[5] While there is a definite case to be made that genocidal doctors are also serial murderers, political and social factors set them apart from other serial killers. Therefore, they have not been included in this book.

Many medical serial killers enjoy having power over life and death.

Medical Serial Killers

It's worth noting that serial killers may have more than one motive for committing their crimes. A power-seeking serial killer, for example, may also be motivated by the prospect of financial gain.

This text explores the minds and deeds of some of the most notorious medical serial killers. What made them killers? What were their motives? And what led to their downfall?

Chapter 1

THE POWER SEEKERS

Power-seeking serial killers have a need to control others, guided by a belief that they are superior to everyone else and thus have the authority to make life-and-death decisions. They may very well have narcissistic personality disorder (NPD), with an inflated sense of their own importance, a desire for admiration, and a lack of empathy for others. Deep down, however, they often suffer from low self-esteem. Female power-seeking serial killers may be responding not just to their own psychological needs, but also to their lower status in society. The power differential between men and women is especially pronounced in the field of health care. Lower-paying jobs such as nursing have historically been filled by women, while doctors were more often likely to be male. (Fortunately, that gender gap is narrowing, and nurses and other health care professionals are gaining more of the respect they deserve.)

Harold Frederick Shipman

aka "Dr. Death"

Born: January 14, 1946

Occupation: Physician

Motive: Power

Arrested: September 7, 1998

Died: January 13, 2004

Dr. Harold Shipman's patients trusted him. Some even adored him. Shipman gladly made house calls to visit his patients, many of them elderly women. He sometimes popped in just to chat with them—or to kill them. Shipman used his reputation as a caring and capable doctor to murder hundreds of people under his care. He might have killed many more, had he not made one uncharacteristic blunder.

Harold Frederick Shipman was one of three children, and he was clearly his mother's favorite. She convinced him that he was better than the other children in his working-class neighborhood in Nottingham, England, and encouraged him to stay home and study and read rather than play with his classmates. He apparently took to heart his mother's belief in his superiority, a hallmark of his psychopathic personality.

When Shipman was in his mid-teens, he watched his mother die of lung cancer. He watched as the family doctor eased her pain with regular shots of morphine until she died. The seventeen-year-old

Shipman, having witnessed firsthand the power that doctors can have over the lives of the ill, decided to go into medicine.

By the time Shipman graduated from medical school in 1970, he had a wife, a young daughter, and a drug habit. He had begun abusing pethidine, a painkiller similar to morphine that gives the user a short-lived high. Investigators believe he began killing his first patients when he was a "junior doctor" (equivalent to a resident in the US medical system) probably by injecting lethal doses of pethidine. Throughout the years, Shipman would continue to use drugs in the morphine family to kill his patients. In the beginning, investigators believe he experimented on ways to kill patients already dying, especially during the evening shifts when few other health care workers were around.[1]

Shipman lost his first job when his colleagues discovered that he had been forging prescriptions for large amounts of pethidine for his own use. He was found guilty of forgery and prescription fraud, and paid a hefty fine. But he wasn't barred from medicine; after doing a stint in a rehabilitation facility, he found a job in 1979 at another group practice in the town of Hyde.

He had a good reputation with his patients, taking an interest in their personal lives even as he kept up with the latest medical breakthroughs. As a result, there was always a waiting list to get onto his roster of patients. He relished in his patients' adoration, convinced that he was by far the best doctor in Hyde. He curried favor toward the other physicians in the practice, but he was aloof and condescending toward coworkers that he thought of as less educated than himself.

Shipman had many of his patients and their families fooled. This is the area where some of his patients recovered after treatment. Others were not so lucky.

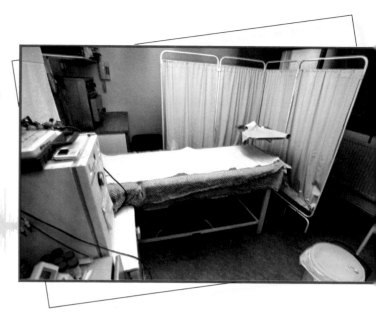

He continued killing patients, most of them elderly, throughout his years at the group practice and then at the private clinic he established in 1992. His patients began dying at even greater numbers. A local taxi driver who often drove elderly patients to Shipman's clinic noted how many of them seemed to die there. He continued his practice of home visits, where many of his patients were later found dead, fully clothed and sitting upright—a pattern that raised a red flag for the local undertaker.

In March of 1998 Dr. Linda Reynolds, prompted by the Frank Massey and Sons Funeral Parlour in Hyde, expressed concerns to the local coroner about the high rate of death among Shipman's patients. Perhaps the most alarming to the coroner was the large number of cremations Shipman sought for his female patients.

Medical Serial Killers

Even as the authorities began investigating the deaths of Shipman's patients, the doctor continued to kill, now often stealing cash and jewelry from the homes of his victims. He was finally caught after murdering an unusually healthy elderly woman named Kathleen Grundy, and forging a crude will in her name that left him her entire fortune. Her daughter was suspicious, and when the woman's body was exhumed and autopsied, authorities found lethal amounts of diamorphine. Other exhumations and autopsies followed, with similar results. He was arrested September 7, 1998, charged with the murder of Grundy and two other people. He was later charged with twelve other murders. The evidence against Shipman was overwhelming, and after a week of deliberation the jury found him guilty for all fifteen murders. He was sentenced to life in prison, and on January 2004, he hanged himself in his cell at Wakefield Prison on the 13th of the same month, one day before his fifty-eighth birthday. He maintained his innocence until the end.

Why did Shipman kill? Despite the petty theft and the will, his primary motivation was clearly not gain, but power. The man had a great sense of superiority, was an accomplished liar, and had a deep-seated need to control people—important hallmarks of the psychopathic personality. Investigators believe that his early drug addiction may also have played a role in his compulsion to kill. "The psychiatrists say that a person who has one addiction is quite likely to be subject to other forms of addiction," wrote Dame Janet Smith in *The Shipman Report*. "I think it likely that whatever it was that caused Shipman to become addicted to pethidine also led to other forms of addictive behavior. It is possible that he was addicted to killing."[2]

Harold Shipman is the only British doctor in history to have been found guilty of murdering his own patients. Eighty percent of his victims were female, and his youngest victim was a forty-one-year-old man. The British legal system surrounding health care and medicine has since been modified and restructured as a result of Shipman's atrocities.

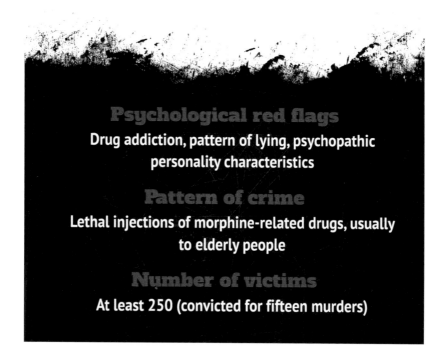

Psychological red flags

Drug addiction, pattern of lying, psychopathic personality characteristics

Pattern of crime

Lethal injections of morphine-related drugs, usually to elderly people

Number of victims

At least 250 (convicted for fifteen murders)

Orville Lynn Majors
aka "The Angel of Death"

Born: **1941**
Occupation: **Licensed practical nurse**
Motive: **Power, missionary killing**
Arrested: **December 29, 1997**

Paula Holdaway held her eighty-year-old mother's hand as she lay in her bed in the intensive care unit (ICU) of the Vermillion County Hospital in Clinton, Indiana. The doctors felt the elderly woman, Dorothea Hixon, was stable and in no immediate danger, but they wanted to keep a close eye on her. Paula watched as Orville Lynn Majors, a licensed practical nurse (LPN), injected something into her mother's intravenous (IV) line, kissed the woman on her forehead, and brushed her hair back.

"It's all right, pumkin," he said. "Everything is going to be all right now pumkin." A minute later, Hixon was dead.[3]

Holdaway was so moved by Major's tenderness in her mother's final moments that she wrote him a thank-you note. To many patients and their families, Majors was a real angel. He was an angel, all right: an Angel of Death.

Born in Kentucky, the son of a coal miner, Orville Lynn Majors developed an interest in health care after caring for his ailing grandmother as a teenager. Later, he and his parents would move

Sheriff's deputies lead Majors out of the courthouse after his arraignment in 1997.

to Linton, Indiana. His parents were well-liked business owners in the small town, and neighbors thought Majors polite and kind.

In 1993, the year Majors was hired at the Vermillion County Hospital, there were 31 deaths in the four-bed ICU, roughly the same as it had been in previous years. In the coming months, it became a kind of in-hospital joke that patients died whenever Majors was on shift. But as patient deaths in the ICU skyrocketed—there would be 101 in 1994—the black humor turned to real concern.

Rumors began to fly that Majors might somehow be involved in the growing number of patient deaths. Finally, in early 1995, the nursing director of the ICU compared the time and date of the deaths with employee's time cards. What she found was shocking: Of the 147 deaths in the ICU between May of 1993 (when Majors began working at the hospital) and December 1994, 130 occurred when Majors was on shift. If Majors was working on a particular day, it was nearly forty-three percent more likely that someone would die in the ICU than if he were not working. When he began working weekend shifts, the deaths shifted to the weekends. There was a break in the run of deaths when Majors went on vacation.

In March of 1995, hospital administrators dismissed Majors and informed the police of their suspicions. The death rate returned to normal as the Indiana State Police launched a criminal investigation that led to Major's arrest in December 1997. Several witnesses said that they had seen Majors inject something into the patients just before they died LPNs are not licensed to give injections). The investigators determined that Majors had probably killed most of his victims with lethal injections of epinephrine and

Seven of Majors' victims were exhumed by the medical examiner to help the state of Indiana build a case against him.

potassium chloride, drugs that cause the heart to speed up and then stop. Police found vials of epinephrine and syringes in his van. They exhumed the bodies of seven suspected victims. Although potassium chloride and epinephrine leave no chemical trace after death, the pathologist who performed the autopsies found that their deaths were consistent with the administration of these drugs.[4]

During the investigation, a darker side of the man generally seen as kind and gentle began to emerge. He told a former room-mate that he hated all old people, saying "they should all be gassed." A former coworker said that he referred to some of his patients and their families as "whiners" and "white trash." One time, when he was asked why he was standing by an elderly woman's bedside, he said that he was "waiting for the woman to die."[5]

Despite Majors' continued protests of innocence, the jury found him guilty in the murder of six people. He was sentenced to six consecutive sixty-year sentences.

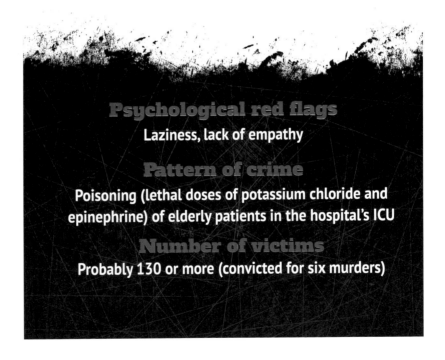

Psychological red flags

Laziness, lack of empathy

Pattern of crime

Poisoning (lethal doses of potassium chloride and epinephrine) of elderly patients in the hospital's ICU

Number of victims

Probably 130 or more (convicted for six murders)

Charles Cullen

Born: **February 22, 1960**
Occupation: **Nurse**
Motive: **Power, attention-seeking, gain**
Arrested: **December 14, 2003**

A deeply unhappy man, Charles Cullen tried—and failed—to commit suicide twenty times. The first attempt would be at the age of nine, when he drank chemicals from a chemistry set. But the man who was so inept at killing himself was surprisingly good at murdering others.

Charles Cullen was the youngest of eight children in a deeply religious Catholic family in West Orange, New Jersey. His father died when he was just seven months old. He felt bullied and helpless in school. When he was seventeen years old, his mother, to whom he was very close, died in a car crash. He dropped out of high school and joined the Navy. He didn't get along with the other sailors, who teased him, calling him "Charlie Fishbelly." He was discharged from the Navy in 1984, after years of increasingly strange behavior and another suicide attempt.

Charles enrolled in nursing school, where he made good grades. By 1987, Charles got his first job as a registered nurse (RN) in the burn unit at St. Barnabas Medical Center in Livingston, New Jersey. But his job and his marriage to his girlfriend did little to calm his demons.

Cullen admitted to four additional murders two years after his initial arrest. Here, on June 25, 2007, he confessed before the Superior Court of Flemington, New Jersey.

In 1988, he killed his first patient, a seventy-two-year-old man, by injecting his IV tube with a lethal dose of a heart drug. Afterwards, he made a show of trying to heroically save the man's life.

Later, Cullen would admit to killing ten more patients at St. Barnabas, before he quit when hospital authorities began to suspect him of tampering with patients' IV bags.

Despite the suspicions of the authorities at St. Barnabas, Cullen soon found a job at nearby Warren Hospital, where he murdered three more elderly women. One of the women's sons accused him of murder, but the hospital investigations were inconclusive. Meanwhile, his marriage had deteriorated. When his wife filed for divorce in 1993, she cited his alcoholism and accused him of domestic violence. He had tortured and killed several of their family pets, she said, and she feared for the safety of herself and their two young daughters.

Cullen went through a series of jobs in the coming years, moving from hospital to hospital, always quitting or being fired under a cloud of suspicion. He preferred working the night shift, which always made him initially popular with the staff, unaware that he liked it because there were few people around to witness his murders. On several occasions, police were called in to investigate, but they could pin nothing on him. Their job was made more difficult by the fact that Cullen often worked on burn or critical care wards, where death was not unusual. By this time, he had adopted a favorite poison: a lethal injection of the heart drug digoxin. Throughout this time, he had a series of failed love affairs and made several suicide attempts.

27

Melissa Hardgrove, daughter to Christopher Hardgrove (in the photo at right), one of Cullen's victims, openly cries during Cullen's sentencing.

When Cullen was arrested on the count of one murder and one attempted murder in December 14, 1993, he confessed that he had killed these victims as well as many more—perhaps forty-five in all. He claimed that he killed the patients to end their suffering, and could not stand to see or hear about attempts to resuscitate the dying.[6] It became clear, however, that many of his victims were not in pain, and in fact were recovering nicely.

Charles Cullen plead guilty to the murder of twenty-two people. He is serving eleven consecutive life terms in New Jersey and seven life terms in Pennsylvania.

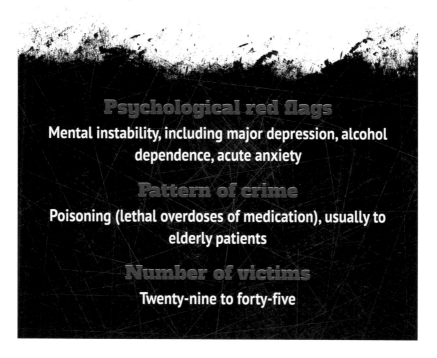

Psychological red flags
Mental instability, including major depression, alcohol dependence, acute anxiety

Pattern of crime
Poisoning (lethal overdoses of medication), usually to elderly patients

Number of victims
Twenty-nine to forty-five

Arnfinn Nesset

Born: **October 25, 1936**
Occupation: **Nurse**
Motive: **Power, financial gain**
Arrested: **January 1981**

Arnfinn Nesset was a mild-mannered, bespectacled, balding man. The nurse and hospital administrator hardly seemed the murderous type. In fact, Nesset's neighbor described him as a "good and helpful man." A midwife who had known Nesset when they were both students said that "he was a very kind student. . . . I never saw him unwilling to help or irritable. That was remarkable since we would put in eight to twelve hours a day."[7] Yet Nesset, Norway's most prolific serial killer, told the police, "I've killed so many I'm unable to remember them all."[8]

Nesset, an illegitimate child, grew up in a small rural community on Norway's west coast. Psychiatrists who examined him suggested that these circumstances made him feel unwanted and isolated as a child. As an adult, the psychiatrists said, he had a deep inferiority complex and a tendency to become aggressive under certain circumstances.[9] He continued to live with his mother long into

his adulthood, and stayed with her in her childhood home, which probably furthered his feelings of isolation.

Arnfinn Nesset became the director of the Orkdal Valley Nursing Home when it opened its doors in 1977. There was a high mortality rate in the facility, but it was, after all, a home for very old people. It wasn't until 1981 that someone raised a red flag: A nursing home employee noticed that Nesset had ordered a large amount of curacit some time in 1980. Curacit, used as a muscle relaxant during surgery, is derived from curare, the lethal poison that South American Indians put on the tips of their arrows. In lethal doses, curacit causes a slow, painful death by suffocation. It breaks down quickly and is difficult to detect after death. The employee, wondering if the high mortality rate might be related to the curacit, contacted local journalists, leading to a police investigation.

Initially, Nesset claimed that he had purchased the curacit to put his dog to sleep. A curious claim, since he did not own a dog and he had ordered enough curacit to kill at least 200 healthy people.[10]

Eventually, Nesset confessed to murdering twenty-seven patients between May 1977 and November 1980, claiming that some were mercy killings—a strange mercy, given the fact that death by curacit is painful and slow. What's more, he said that he got sexual pleasure from the act of killing.

Following Nesset's confession, police looked into the deaths of patients at three other facilities where he had worked since 1962. Investigators determined that he had probably killed at least sixty-two people.

Nesset was charged with killing twenty-five patients at the Orkdal Valley Nursing Home. Shortly before his trial, he recanted

The Orkdal Nursing Home in Oslo, Norway was Nesset's hunting ground.

his confession, saying that he had been "confused in the head." The court didn't buy his claim—especially given the fact that he had also stolen about $1,800 from some of his victims. On March 11, 1983, Nesset was convicted on twenty-two counts of murder, one count of attempted murder, and a number of forgery and embezzlement charges. He was sentenced to twenty-one years in prison, the maximum allowed under Norwegian law. He spent twelve years in prison, and ten years under supersvision (on probation in the

American legaly system). He was released in 2004 and is presumed to be living under a new name somewhere in Norway.

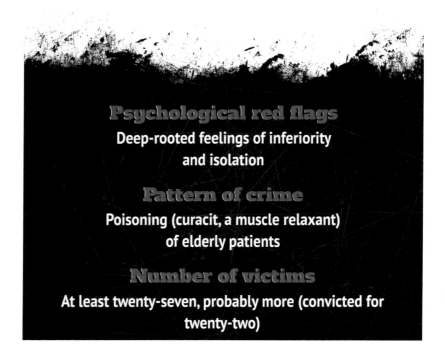

Psychological red flags
Deep-rooted feelings of inferiority
and isolation

Pattern of crime
Poisoning (curacit, a muscle relaxant)
of elderly patients

Number of victims
At least twenty-seven, probably more (convicted for
twenty-two)

Waltraud Wagner

one of four "Lainz Angels of Death"

Born: 1960
Occupation: Nurse's aide
Motive: Power
Arrested: April 7, 1989

Waltraud Wagner, the sadistic ringleader of a murderous group of nurse's aides known as the Lainz Angels of Death, was forthright about her motive for killing patients under her care. "The ones who got on my nerves," she told Austrian authorities, "were dispatched directly to a free bed with the good Lord."[11]

There is little about Wagner's early life to indicate that she would become a serial killer. One of six children, Wagner grew up on a farm in a rural part of Austria. By the age of twelve, she was helping care for her ailing grandmother. She failed nursing school because she couldn't pass her anatomy course, but she was able to get a job as a nurse's aide at Lainz General Hospital in Vienna, Austria. She was assigned to the graveyard shift in an overcrowded ward reserved for elderly patients. It was often a difficult job, but supervisors described her as a hard worker. She was a natural leader, charming, and always willing to take charge of the situation.[12]

Medical Serial Killers

In 1983, a seventy-seven-year-old woman asked Wagner to help end her suffering. The take-charge aide gave the woman a fatal dose of morphine—and experienced a surge of power and excitement. She couldn't believe how easy it was—and nobody suspected a thing. The woman had been dying, after all. Wagner, only twenty-three years old at the time, soon recruited other nurse aides, all working the night shift, to join her in a campaign of so-called mercy killing. Her first recruits, Maria Gruber, nineteen, and Irene Leidolf, twenty-one, quickly fell under the sway of their older, more charismatic supervisor. Stefanie Mayer, forty-three, soon joined the little gang of killers. Mayer was a recent hire whose low self-esteem and a divorce after a difficult marriage left her easily manipulated.[13]

Wagner showed the other aides how to give lethal injections of insulin and morphine. After a time, she developed another, more brutal form of murder: the "water cure." This involved holding a patient's nose and pouring water down the throat. The patients essentially drowned as their lungs filled with water—a slow, painful death. The "water cure" deaths attracted little attention, since it is common for frail, elderly people to die with fluid in their lungs.

At first, Wagner and her team targeted people who were already at death's door, convincing themselves that they were carrying out acts of mercy. Soon they moved on to patients who annoyed Wagner, whether by snoring too loudly, soiling bedsheets, or buzzing the nurse's station for help at inconvenient times. Any patient who complained about her soon ended up in the morgue. Although Wagner orchestrated the murders, she often delegated the actual act of killing to the other aides. The other aides both

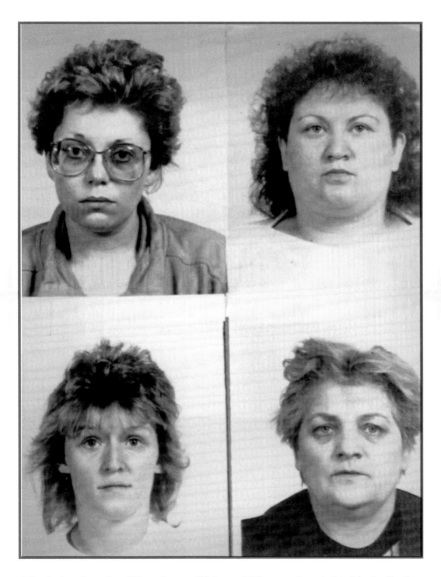

The Lainz Angels of Death are: Waltraud Wagner (top left), Maria Gruber (top right), Irene Leidolf (bottom left), and Stefanie Mayer (bottom right).

admired and feared Wagner: They knew that people who annoyed her tended to die.

By 1988, the death rate in the ward was so high that it became known as the "death pavilion."[14] Despite widespread rumors of a killer at large on Pavilion 5, there was no investigation.

The aides had gotten into the habit of meeting for drinks after their shift, recounting their exploits. One day in February 1989, having had perhaps a few too many drinks, they were laughing about the death of a woman who had received the "water cure" after complaining about Wagner. A doctor sitting nearby overheard their conversation. Remembering the rumors, he notified the police. A six-week investigation led to the arrest of the four women on April 7.

Wagner confessed to killing thirty-nine people, even naming the method of killing in each case. When investigators asked her how she could recall those details, she winked and said, "You'd remember something like this!"[15] The three other women confessed to ten murders each. Further investigations revealed that the murder count may have been closer to 300.

In February 1991, Wagner was convicted of fifteen murders, seventeen attempted murders, and two counts of assault. She was sentenced to life in prison. Liedolf was convicted of five murders, also receiving life in prison. Gruber and Mayer each received fifteen years in prison for manslaughter and attempted murder.

Wagner and Leidolf were released in 2008 for good behavior. The other two aides were released some time earlier. All four are believed to be living under new identities.

Irene Leidolf testifies in court on March 3, 1991.It was Austria's biggest murder trial since World War II.

Psychological red flags

Possibly influenced by caring for her ailing grandmother; definitely craved power over patients and colleagues

Pattern of crime

Poisoning (morphine, insulin) and drowning of elderly patients

Number of victims

Probably close to 300 (Waltraud was convicted of fifteen murders)

Efren Saldivar
aka "The Angel of Death"

Born: September 30, 1969
Occupation: Respiratory therapist
Motive: Power
Arrested: January 19, 2001

Efren Saldivar, a respiratory therapist at Glendale Adventist Medical Center in southern California, lost count of the patients he murdered. After confessing to killing patients to ease his workload, he told detectives, "It was a gradual thing ... I did it without thinking. I don't know if you ever shoplifted a piece of gum or something. You don't plan it. After that moment, you don't think about it for the rest of the day, or ever."[16]

Saldivar was born in Brownsville, Texas, the son of Mexican immigrant parents seeking a better life in the United States. The family moved to the Los Angeles area when the boy was not yet two years old. His parents were hard workers, and he attended church every Sunday with his mother. As a teen, he was outgoing, yet socially awkward, especially around girls. A self-professed "goody-goody," he secretly wished to be a part of a gang, "doing drugs and looking cool and being tough."[17]

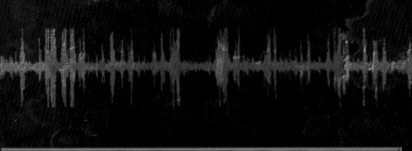

Saldivar appears at the Glendale Superior Court in California on January 11, 2001.

Saldivar was intelligent, but he didn't apply himself in school, and failed to graduate. He worked at a local supermarket until a friend, recently graduated from trade school, showed up wearing his hospital uniform. Soon, he earned a high school equivalency degree and trained to become a respiratory therapist. Later, someone asked Saldivar if he entered the medical profession because he wanted to help people. Not at all, he said. He liked the uniform. In his eyes, a uniform gave him the status he craved—and power. He learned to use a syringe to withdraw blood from the arms of patients to test their oxygen levels, and enjoyed the feeling of watching patients improve after he gave them lung treatments.

Saldivar preferred the night shift, when few other staff were on duty. Most of his colleagues thought him competent, if at times a bit lazy. Still, he was good with computers and was always happy to help staff members with their software problems.

The killings began about six months after Saldivar started working at the hospital in 1989. As he would later tell investigators, his first victim was a patient dying of cancer. He turned off the patient's respirator. "The patient basically suffocated," he told police.[18]

Over time, Salvidar switched to injecting his victims with Pavulon, a paralytic drug commonly used to stop a patient's respiration as they are about to be put on a ventilator. He was no random killer, at least not at first. His targets had to be unconscious, they had to have a "do not resuscitate" (DNR) order, and they had to look like they were ready to die. One investigator said, "He talked about his anger at seeing patients kept alive as opposed to the guilt he would feel at the failure to provide life-saving care," and considered himself an "angel of death."[19] The killings went on for about eight years, but since his victims were near death anyway, they went largely unnoticed.

Still, colleagues reported that Salvidar would say that a certain patient needed to die—and then that patient would die that very night. They joked that he had a "magic syringe." When some other respiratory technicians discovered Pavulon, other drugs, and syringes in Salvidar's locker, it seemed that his "magic syringe" was indeed real.

When the police brought Salvidar in for questioning, he confessed to killing forty or fifty patients—those he believed were "ready to die."[20] But investigators were unable to find any evidence to confirm Salvidar's confession, and were forced to release him

Jean Coyle (right), is one of the only known survivors of Saldivar.

forty-eight hours later. When his confession was made public, Salvidar was fired from his job, and his respiratory therapist's license was taken away. He soon took back his confession, saying that he was depressed and wanted to die, hoping that he would receive the death penalty.

Investigators stepped up their efforts to find physical evidence of the murders, sorting through the records of people who had died under Salvidar's watch. They identified twenty potential victims, and dug them out of their graves. Pathologists found traces of Pavulon in six of the bodies. Salvidar was finally arrested for the murder of six people in January 2001. He was sentenced to six consecutive life sentences without the possibility of parole. Investigators later found that Salvidar probably murdered close to 200 people.

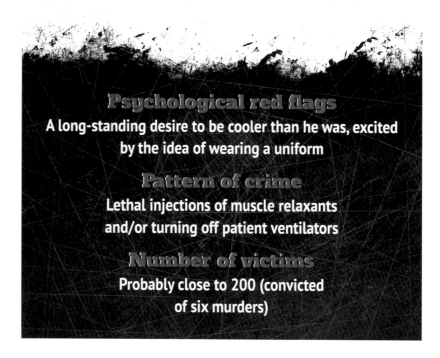

Psychological red flags

A long-standing desire to be cooler than he was, excited by the idea of wearing a uniform

Pattern of crime

Lethal injections of muscle relaxants and/or turning off patient ventilators

Number of victims

Probably close to 200 (convicted of six murders)

Donald Harvey
aka " The Angel of Death"

Born: **April 15, 1952**

Occupation: **Hospital orderly**

Motive: **Power**

Arrested: **April 1987**

Donald Harvey, arguably the most prolific serial killer in the United States, relished power. When a reporter asked him why he killed, he answered, "Well, people controlled me for 18 years, and then I controlled my own destiny. I controlled other people's lives, whether they lived or died. I had that power to control.... I appointed myself judge, prosecutor and jury. So I played God."[21]

Harvey, an only child, grew up in a tiny town in Kentucky. Although his mother described him as a "good boy," his childhood was marked by trauma. By the time he was five years old, he had suffered two head injuries, one occurring when he was just an infant. Worse, his uncle began molesting him when he was just four years old. A male neighbor started sexually abusing him just a year later. The two men would take turns with Harvey over the next fifteen years.[22] It is not clear whether Harvey's head injuries were in any way associated with his psychopathic personality, but the years of sexual abuse almost certainly contributed to his lifelong depression and a deep hunger to control the lives of others.

Donald Harvey stands before a judge during sentencing in Cincinnati, Ohio, September 1987.

Harvey was intelligent but easily bored in school. He dropped out of high school when he was sixteen, easily earning his general equivalency diploma (GED) in 1968. After losing his factory job, he found a job as an orderly at Marymount Hospital in London, Kentucky in 1970. He changed bedpans, mopped floors, and passed out medications.

His first victim was Logan Evans. Evans, an eighty-eight-year-old stroke patient suffering from dementia, smeared feces on Harvey's face. Harvey snapped, smothering the old man with a sheet of plastic and a pillow. Afterwards, Harvey cleaned himself and his victim, and dressed Evans in a clean hospital gown. "No one ever questioned it," Harvey recalled.[23]

Harvey remained at Marymount Hospital for nearly a year, killing as many as thirteen people. Unlike many serial killers, he experimented with a variety of different methods: suffocation, disconnecting oxygen tanks, and injecting lethal substances such as arsenic and cyanide. In one case, he stuck a straightened coat hanger into his victim's catheter, puncturing the man's bladder and bowel. The man died of an infection a few days later.

The killings stopped for a few years. After he was arrested for an attempted burglary, he enlisted in the Air Force, perhaps in an effort to get his life back on track. It didn't go well: he was given a general discharge after less than a year. Severely depressed, he tried to kill himself. He was committed to a mental hospital, where he received a series of electroshock treatments.

After Harvey's discharge in 1972, he took jobs in a series of hospitals in Kentucky and Ohio. The killings resumed in 1975—this time, both in and out of the hospital. He poisoned his boyfriend,

Harvey is led back to jail in London, Kentucky, November 2, 1987, after pleading guilty to eight counts of murder and one count of voluntary manslaughter.

whom he suspected was seeing other men. He would slip a small dose of arsenic into his lover's meal, just enough to keep him sick at home the next day. He fatally poisoned a meddlesome neighbor, his boyfriend's father, and his boyfriend's brother-in-law. He tried, and failed, to poison his boyfriend's mother.

Harvey continued killing until April 1987. The pathologist performing an autopsy on a patient named John Powell noticed the faint scent of almonds—the hallmark of cyanide poisoning. Suspicious, he notified the authorities, whose investigations led them to Harvey. In August of that year, he confessed to committing thirty-three murders over the past seventeen years. He would later claim that the number was seventy, or maybe eighty. In the end, thirty-seven murders were actually confirmed, making him the most prolific serial killer in the United States. A psychiatrist who examined Harvey said that he was legally sane, and compulsively killed to relieve his unbearable tension. Harvey was convicted of twenty-four murders, and four attempted murders, and sentenced to life in prison. He will be eligible for parole in 2048, at age ninety-six.

A true psychopath, Harvey placed the blame on others for his crimes. He told an interviewer that the various hospitals should have caught him, but that overworked doctors never bothered to visit patients after they died.

Psychological red flags
Childhood sexual abuse, severe mental
illness, including depression

Pattern of crime
Suffocation, poisoning, disconnecting
oxygen tanks; victims included patients
as well as personal acquaintances

Number of victims
Seventy to eighty; thirty-seven confirmed

Chapter 2

THE COMFORT-ORIENTED HEDONISTS

Health care providers are uniquely positioned to take financial advantage of their most vulnerable patients. Caregivers may use their superficial charm and warmth to persuade their grateful patients to name them as beneficiaries in their insurance policies or include them into their wills. Many, but not all, comfort-oriented hedonist serial killers are female, targeting people they know quite well.

Some comfort killers seek emotional, rather than financial, gain. Some just like being the center of attention whenever their patient dies. Other attention-seekers may have some form of Munchausen Syndrome by Proxy. People with this condition cause life-threatening symptoms in their victims, usually their own children. They revel in the attention and sympathy of the medical staff trying to save the child's life, and the importance they feel as the child's protector. In the case of the health care professionals with this syndrome, they create medical emergencies so that they can heroically save the child and bask in the praise for their efforts.

Munchausen Syndrome by Proxy is different from the classic Munchausen Syndrome, which often begins in childhood or adolescence. A person with Munchausen Syndrome fakes an illness, or even makes herself sick, to get attention and sympathy. Munchausen Syndrome is often a precursor to Munchausen Syndrome by Proxy. The term "Munchausen Syndrome" comes from an eighteenth-century literary character based on a German officer named Baron Munchausen who happened to be a great storyteller. The fictional "Baron Munchausen" was not just a storyteller, he told extravagant lies and exaggerations about his adventures.[1]

Thomas Neill Cream
aka "The Lambeth Poisoner"

Born: **May 27, 1850**
Occupation: **Physician/surgeon**
Motive: **Financial gain, missionary**
Arrested: **July 13, 1892**
Died: **November 15, 1892**

Thomas Neill Cream might very well have gotten away with his murders had it not been for his own greed and an ego-driven compulsion to meddle in the investigations of those deaths.

Cream was born in Glasgow, Scotland in 1850, but moved to Quebec, Canada, with his family when he was just four years old. The eldest of eight children, he was an unusually bright young man. Although his father had built a thriving lumber business in Canada, Thomas had his sights set on the medical profession.

And so, in 1872, Thomas began his medical studies at McGill University in Montreal, Canada. Despite his intelligence, he was only an average student. He had an above-average interest in drugs, however: He wrote his doctoral thesis on chloroform. A popular anesthetic at the time, chloroform was known to be potentially deadly in higher doses.

After graduating with his medical degree in 1876, Thomas set fire to his lodgings, claiming the $350 in insurance money from the

Scottish-born Thomas Cream is thought to have been responsible

damage—an early indication of the greed that would accompany many of his later crimes. He impregnated, and then performed an abortion on, a young woman he had been seeing. Their affair came to light when the woman became very ill following the abortion. Cream was forced to marry the woman, more or less at gunpoint. He left for England shortly after their wedding, leaving his wife behind in Canada. Less than a year after their marriage, his wife died from an overdose after taking some pills he had sent her. This was probably his first murder.

Cream continued his studies in London and Edinburgh, and returned to Canada. He developed a thriving and legitimate medical practice in London, Ontario, performing illegal abortions on the side. In May 1879, the body of a young, pregnant woman was found outside his office. The cause of death was determined to be chloroform poisoning. Police suspected Cream, but they couldn't pin the murder on him. Still, he thought it best to relocate his abortion practice—this time, just outside the red light district in Chicago, Illinois. He killed at least two of his patients, giving strychnine pills to one and botching the abortion of another. Strychnine, often used as a rat poison, causes an excruciating death.

Meanwhile, Cream was having an affair with a woman named Julia Stott. In 1881, Cream slipped some strychnine into the epilepsy medicine he had prescribed for Stott's husband. Cream might have gotten away with the murder had he not written a letter to the coroner, accusing the pharmacist of poisoning Mr. Stott. Sure enough, when the authorities dug up the body, it was clear that the man had been murdered. But an investigation revealed that it was Cream, not the pharmacist, who had poisoned Mr. Stott. Cream was sentenced to life in prison in Illinois, but he was released ten years later, after bribing politicians for a pardon.

Cream boarded a ship bound for England, arriving in London on October 7, 1891. He wasted no time. On October 13, he gave a nineteen-year-old prostitute a drink laced with strychnine and morphine. In the agonizing moments before her death, Ellen Donworth described her killer: "a cross-eyed man with a silk hat and bushy moustache."[2]

Ever greedy, Cream wrote a letter to the deputy coroner under the pseudonym Detective O'Brien, promising to find the killer in exchange for a large amount of money.

Just two days later he used strychnine to kill Matilda Clover, also a prostitute. He had written her a letter—a piece of evidence that would later be used to convict him. He gave another prostitute, Lou Harvey, some pills that he claimed would cure some spots on her forehead. Suspicious, she pretended to take the pills and threw them away. After two more prostitutes died of strychnine poisoning, the police knew they had a serial killer on their hands.

Meanwhile, Cream wrote blackmail letters to two different people, claiming he had evidence that *they* were involved in the murders. He befriended a retired detective, and thinking that since the man was retired, his confession was safe, he described the murders in great detail. Cream even took the retired detective on a tour of the murder sites. He talked at length about his victims, including Lou Harvey, who he presumed was dead. The detective contacted Scotland Yard.

Harvey, who was alive and well, confirmed that Cream had tried to get her to take some pills. Investigators were able to match the

Illustrated above is the alleged tenth Jack the Ripper murder in Whitechapel, London. Although five murders are widely believed to be linked to the Ripper, some people think that other killings in the area were his handywork as well.

Was Thomas Neill Cream the Real Jack the Ripper?

Cream's last words were reported to have been, "I am Jack—," his sentence cut short as his neck snapped in the hangman's noose. These words led (and still lead) people to speculate that he was confessing to being Jack the Ripper, the notorious murderer of five London prostitutes in 1888. Could Cream have been Jack the Ripper, or were his words the psychopath's final attempt to grab the attention of the world?

Consider the evidence in support of the Cream-as-Ripper theory:

- Both targeted prostitutes.
- Both wrote letters to the authorities boasting about the murders.
- Both used particularly cruel methods of killing their victims.
- Like Cream, Jack the Ripper seemed to have some medical knowledge.

Evidence against the Cream-as-Ripper theory:

- Cream was in prison just outside of Chicago when the Ripper murders occurred. (Those who believe Cream may have been Jack the Ripper point out that it was not uncommon for prisoners, especially wealthy ones, to pay other people to serve their time for them. Given the corruption in Chicago in the 1880s, this is not too far-fetched.)
- The killers used very different methods: Cream poisoned his victims, while Jack the Ripper strangled and then butchered his victims.

handwriting in the letter he wrote to Clover with the blackmail letters.

Cream was found guilty for the murder of the four London prostitutes. He was executed by hanging on November 15, 1892.

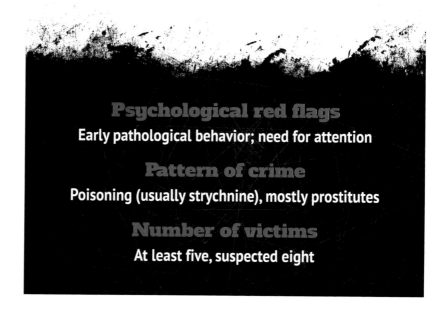

Psychological red flags

Early pathological behavior; need for attention

Pattern of crime

Poisoning (usually strychnine), mostly prostitutes

Number of victims

At least five, suspected eight

H. H. Holmes
aka "America's First Serial Killer"

Born: **May 16, 1861**
Occupation: **Physician**
Motive: **Financial gain, thrill**
Arrested: **November 17, 1894**
Died: **May 7, 1896**

In Dr. H. H. Holmes' confession to the murder of twenty-seven people, he wrote, "I was born with the devil in me. I could not help the fact that I was a murderer, no more than the poet can help the inspiration to sing."[3] Given the horrific nature of his crimes, it is not hard to believe that he was telling the truth.

H. H. Holmes was born Herman Webster Mudgett in New Hampshire in 1861. His family was quite religious, and his father, a farmer, regularly beat him when he misbehaved. Other children bullied him. When Mudgett was five years old, some older boys dragged him into a doctor's office and placed him in front of a skeleton. They had hoped to frighten the boy, but he was fascinated. He would later say that this incident led to his decision to become a doctor.

Like many serial killers and psychopaths, Mudgett tortured and killed small animals. He would dissect them while they were still alive, or stretch them to the breaking point and cut their ligaments—a technique that he would later use on his human victims.

H.H. Holmes is considered by many to be America's first serial killer.

Mudgett also had the charm so characteristic of psychopaths, and when he was eighteen, he eloped with a young woman named Clara Lovering. He entered medical school a year later, where he used corpses stolen from the hospital and cemetery to defraud life insurance companies. After a series of these and other crimes, his reputation was in tatters. He changed his name to Henry Howard Holmes and left his wife and baby. He never divorced her, but would marry a number of other women for their money. He took a number of odd jobs, leaving several dead people in his wake.

Holmes moved to Englewood, a booming suburb of Chicago, in 1886. He got a job as a chemist in a pharmacy there. He used his considerable charm to persuade the owner of the store, a recent widow, to sell him the business. He offered to let her live upstairs. She disappeared in 1887, and although he told people that she moved to California, she was never seen again. Holmes became very wealthy, in part by selling fake cures to gullible clients. He used his money to build a grand three-story castle. Billed as a hotel, it was in reality an elaborate torture chamber, with secret soundproof chambers, hidden passageways, trapdoors and chutes, and a dissecting room.

When the castle was completed in 1890, Holmes began to kill in earnest. He pumped deadly gas into the rooms of some of his victims, watching them through a peephole. He locked others in a bank vault and allowed them to suffocate. Rooms lined with asbestos were used to burn his victims alive. He stretched some of his victims on his so-called elasticity determinator, recalling his childhood torture of animals. He performed illegal abortions on hundreds of women in other parts of the castle; some of them died. He disposed of some of his victims in vats of acid, selling the bleached skeletons to medical schools. Others were burned in a human-sized oven. He had persuaded many of his victims to take out life insurance policies, naming him as the beneficiary.

Following the World's Fair in 1893, Holmes fled Chicago, leaving a trail of dead bodies as he traveled around the United States and Canada. At one point, Holmes hired a carpenter named Benjamin Pitezel to do some work for him. He persuaded Pitezel to take out a life insurance policy naming Holmes as the beneficiary. The plan

Holmes' murder castle was built for the sole purpose of attracting, torturing, and murdering victims during the Chicago World's Fair in 1893.

was to fake his death so that they could collect and split the money. When the scam fell through, Holmes killed Pitezel and three of his children and tried to claim the money. He was arrested after police discovered the scheme.

Eventually Holmes confessed to killing twenty-seven people, although investigators believe he may have killed as many as 230.[4] He was found guilty of murder and executed by hanging on May 7, 1896.

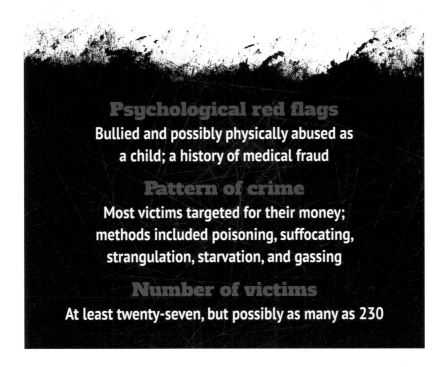

Psychological red flags

Bullied and possibly physically abused as a child; a history of medical fraud

Pattern of crime

Most victims targeted for their money; methods included poisoning, suffocating, strangulation, starvation, and gassing

Number of victims

At least twenty-seven, but possibly as many as 230

Anna Marie Hahn

aka "Arsenic Anna" and
"The Blonde Borgia"

Born: July 7, 1906
Occupation: Live-in health care attendant
Motive: Financial gain
Arrested: September 1937
Died: December 7, 1938

The arrest and trial of Anna Marie Hahn, the first woman to die in Ohio's electric chair, sparked a national media frenzy. The press dubbed the young, pretty woman "The Blonde Borgia," in reference to Lucrezia Borgia, the beautiful Renaissance-era Italian noblewoman said to have been a poisoner. One Cincinnati, Ohio, news reporter described the investigation "one of the most amazing police cases in the history of the city."[5]

Anna Marie Filser, the youngest of twelve children, was her mother's favorite, a little spoiled and rebellious. When she was eighteen years old, she gave birth to a son out of wedlock—quite a scandal in their small Bavarian town. In 1929, she left her three-year-old son with her parents to start a new life where no one knew of her scandalous past.

She lived with her aunt and uncle in the German District of Cincinnati for a month, but moved out quite suddenly without

No. 214, Mrs. Anna Marie Hahn

of Hamilton County, Legally Electrocuted December 7th, 1938, for the Murder of Mr. Jacob Wagner, at Cincinnati, Ohio.

arie Hahn wa   to be execu
ution in Ohio.

paying them the $236 owed them for her boat passage.[6] She worked as a chambermaid, but she always needed more money.

She befriended an elderly banker, Charles Osswald, whose wife had recently died. Filser, who claimed to have nursing experience, became "Uncle Charlie's" caretaker. She persuaded him to transfer his stock shares into her name, after leading him to believe that she would marry him one day. Now she had the money to spend on her real love: betting on horse races. She hoped to win enough to bring her son Oscar to the United States. She had no intention of marrying the old man, of course. Instead, she married twenty-six-year-old Philip Hahn in 1930. Shortly after that, Filser—now Hahn—went to Germany to bring her five-year-old son back to the United States.

When Osswald died of natural causes in 1935, she received a check for $1,000 as the beneficiary of his insurance policy. She had spent all the rest of "Uncle Charlie's" money.

Hahn's first victim was most likely Ernst Kohler, who hired her as his housekeeper in 1932. Hahn, along with her husband and son, rented rooms in Kohler's huge house. She was so charming that after knowing her for just a few weeks, Kohler wrote her into his will. Although it remains unproven, Hahn probably killed him with a lethal dose of morphine, obtained by stealing prescription pads from the doctor's office in the first floor of the house. She inherited the house, all its furnishings, and $13,000.

By this time, it seems that Mr. Hahn understood his wife's ruthlessness when it came to money. And so, when she tried to persuade him to take out a $25,000 life insurance policy, naming her as the beneficiary, he refused. He became very sick soon after. Although Anna claimed she could nurse her husband at home, his mother insisted on taking him to the hospital. The doctors saved his life, and although the Hahns remained married, he avoided her whenever possible.

Hahn's next client was seventy-two-year-old Albert Palmer. She didn't manage to wrangle a will out of him, but she did persuade him to "loan" her a large sum of money, calling him "my dear, sweet Daddy."[7] When he called in the loan in 1937, she put a lethal dose of arsenic in his dinner.

That same year, Hahn showed up at the home of Jacob Wagner, a seventy-eight-year-old retired gardener. Hahn claimed to be his niece, which was news to the old man. But she charmed her way into his life anyway. Two weeks later, the old man died after Hahn gave him a poisoned glass of juice. The next day, a will turned up. Written in English (which Wagner had never learned to do), the will left Hahn $17,000. Handwriting experts would later confirm that Hahn herself wrote the will.[8]

Hahn's fourth victim was George Gsellman, who left Hahn $15,000 after he died in 1937. She had put enough arsenic in his food to kill dozens of people. Finally, Hahn convinced sixty-seven-year-old widower George Obendoerfer to take the train to Colorado with her, along with her son. The three of them, she promised him, would live together on a ranch. By the time they reached Colorado Springs, her mark was deathly ill. She took him to the hospital, where she claimed not to know him. The authorities became suspicious. When Obendoerfer died, an autopsy revealed high levels of arsenic in the man's body.

Although Hahn had first claimed not to know Obendoerfer, she was soon forced to admit that they were together on the train. She claimed that they were only casual friends. It was only a coincidence that they happened to be on the same train. Her story unraveled when the police questioned her eleven-year-old son, who confirmed that Hahn had bought Obendoerfer's ticket at the train station.

Hahn was charged with the murder of Jacob Wagner (Obendoerfer died in Colorado, and investigators wanted to try her in Ohio). A jury found her guilty, and on December 7, 1938, Anna Marie Hahn was executed in the electric chair.

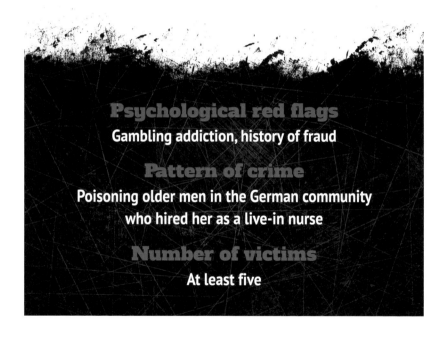

Psychological red flags

Gambling addiction, history of fraud

Pattern of crime

Poisoning older men in the German community
who hired her as a live-in nurse

Number of victims

At least five

Cecile Bombeek
aka "Sister Godfrida"

Born: 1933
Occupation: Nurse/hospital geriatrics manager
Motive: Financial gain
Arrested: February 14, 1978

By all accounts, Cecile Bombeek had once been an excellent nurse. Although there is little information about Bombeek's childhood, we do know that she was raised in a staunchly Catholic home. She took the name Sister Godfrida after taking her vows as a nun, and was the head nurse of the thirty-eight-bed geriatric wing of a hospital in Wetteren, Belgium.

Bombeek's behavior changed drastically after she underwent surgery to remove a brain tumor in 1975.[9] She developed chronic, severe headaches. She became addicted to the morphine used to treat her illness. Two years later, other nurses on the ward began to notice a higher-than-normal death rate. (twenty-one patients in less than a year) There were also disturbing signs of mistreatment, including roughly yanking patients' catheter tubes out of their bladders. They began keeping a diary, noting the shifts when deaths and abuse occurred, and who worked those shifts. The nurses were horrified when it became clear that the common element in all the cases was their very own cherub-faced, plump Sister Godfrida.

At first, hospital officials tried to deal with the problem by sending Bombeek to a drug rehabilitation program, guessing that addiction lay at the root of Bombeek's behavior. Rehab did not work for Bombeek, however, and when she continued to express interest in working at the hospital, they confronted her with the evidence of her crimes.

Bombeek confessed to killing three elderly people by injecting them with overdoses of insulin because they had been "too difficult at night."[10] She insisted, however, that she did it "sweetly," and that none of her victims had suffered. A member of the hospital's governing board acknowledged there may have been many more victims: "It could just as well be 30 people as three."[11]

Investigators found that she also managed to embezzle more than $30,000 from her patients in a year's time. She used that money not just to support her drug habit, but an increasingly lavish lifestyle as well. She was rumored to be having an affair with her roommate, also a nun, and with a retired priest. Bombeek and her lovers dined out at pricey restaurants. Local merchants recalled that the women often had expensive cuts of meat, fresh seafood, and fine wines delivered to their beautifully decorated apartment.

In 1978, Bombeek underwent a psychiatric evaluation. She was found not fit to stand trial, and was committed to an institution on August 28th of that same year. Although her crimes barely fit the perameters befitting a serial murderer, it is one of just a few recorded cases of serial murder commited by a female in Belgium.

Whether her crimes were fueled solely by her addiction and her need for money or some physical damage to her brain caused by the tumor or the surgery may never be known.

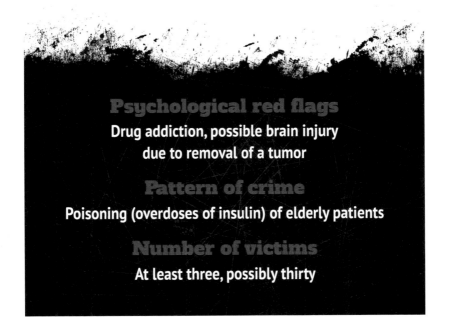

Psychological red flags

**Drug addiction, possible brain injury
due to removal of a tumor**

Pattern of crime

Poisoning (overdoses of insulin) of elderly patients

Number of victims

At least three, possibly thirty

Amelia Dyer
aka "The Reading Baby Farmer"

Born: **1839**
Occupation: **Nurse**
Motive: **Financial gain**
Arrested: **April 4, 1896**
Died: **June 10, 1896**

'Married couple with no family would adopt healthy child, nice country home. Terms, £10."[12]

The advertisement seemed a godsend to twenty-five-year-old Evelina Marmon. The young woman had a two-month-old baby girl named Doris that she loved, but could not care for. Like many unwed mothers at the time, she felt that her only option was to place her baby in foster care. She hoped to pay for her daughter's care in installments, so that she could reclaim her child when her circumstances improved. This practice, sometimes known as "baby farming," was not uncommon in nineteenth-century England.

Instead, "Mrs. Harding," the prospective adoptive mother, insisted on a full adoption with the full payment of £10. The desperate mother reluctantly agreed. Despite the adoptive mother's assurances to the contrary, Marmon never saw her daughter again.[13] She had left her daughter with a woman who would become one of nineteenth-century England's most notorious serial killers: Amelia Dyer.

Rogues Gallery

---WANTED---

AMELIA DYER
BABY MURDERER

Amelia Dyer (born 1838) was a midwife, who knew that once her fee had been paid mothers were rarely interested in their infants' welfare (and fathers less so) she at first tended to neglect sicklier babies, allowing them to die of starvation, but over time assumed the practice of simply strangling babies as soon as she had pocketed the fee and the mother had departed. It was peace of mind they were paying for after all, the children's welfare barely seemed to matter. Killing them was simply cheaper.

Suspicions were raised when the tiny corpses of her victims were found in the Thames, their throats bound with white dressmaking tape. When detectives raided her home they said it stank of decomposing bodies.

While Amelia Dyer pleaded guilty to a single murder, she had committed many more. Perhaps up to 400, placing her among the most prolific killers of all time. She was hanged at Newgate Prison on Wednesday, June 10, 1896.

 # DEAD OR ALIVE

Amelia Dyer was responsible for the deaths of many innocent babies.

Medical Serial Killers

Amelia Elizabeth Hobley was born in a small village near Bristol, England. Details about her childhood are sketchy, but it is known that she was the youngest of five children. Her father was a shoemaker. While the family was not wealthy, they had the means to give Amelia an education. Unlike many girls of her time, she learned how to read and write. Amelia's childhood was marred by her mother's severe mental illness, however, and her mother died when she was just nine years old.

In 1861, at the age of twenty-four, Amelia married a much older man, George Thomas Dyer. She became a nurse, which was a respectable job in Victorian England. When her husband died, she looked for a source of income that would be more lucrative and allow her to care for their daughter, Polly. She found it in baby farming. It took a lot of work and money to care for the infants, and so she began letting her charges starve to death. Sometimes she gave them opium, which had the effect of quieting the hungry babies and hastening their deaths. Soon, she began killing the babies she received outright. She would strangle the babies with a length of white seamstress's tape, put them in bags, and throw them in the river.

When Polly wanted to know what happened to all of the babies, Dyer told her daughter that "she was sending little children to Jesus … because He wanted them far more than their mothers did."[14]

At one point, Dyer did hard labor in a prison for neglecting her charges. Afterwards, she was in and out of mental institutions. Whether she was actually mentally ill or merely in need of a place to lay low is a matter of dispute. But the murders inevitably resumed—for a total of thirty years. The adult Polly and her husband became accomplices, helping Dyer dispose of the bodies. This string of murders was made possible by the complete lack of government regulations or oversight concerning baby farms. Many of the unwed mothers were too ashamed and embarrassed to check in on the well-being of their babies.

Dyer's murderous career came to an end in 1896, when a bargeman found a package containing the body of a baby girl floating in the Thames River. The package had a name and address that would eventually be traced back to Dyer. Investigators dragged the river and found the bodies of dozens of infants. Amelia helpfully told the police, "You'll know all mine by the tape around their necks."[15]

Dyer was charged with the murders of two babies, including Doris Marmon, fished from the Thames River. The true number of Dyer's victims is estimated to be closer to 300. Despite her plea of insanity, Dyer was found guilty and hanged at Newgate Prison.

Psychological red flags
Lost mother to mental illness at a young age

Pattern of crime
Starvation plus opium, strangulation of infants

Number of victims
Estimated to be around 300

Newgate Prison, London, housed many notorious criminals during the 18th and 19th centuries. It closed in 1902.

Marcel Petiot
aka "The Butcher of Paris"

Born: **January 17, 1897**
Occupation: **Physician**
Motive: **Financial gain**
Arrested: **October 31, 1944**
Died: **May 25, 1946**

Life under the Nazi occupation of France during World War II was, for most French citizens, a nightmare. It was even worse for French Jews, of course, who faced deportation to concentration camps. So when a man who went by the code name "Dr. Eugène" let it be known that he could arrange for safe passage out of the country to Argentina, there were plenty of people willing to pay the hefty fee. When the desperate would-be fugitives came to his house with the money and all of the worldly possessions they could carry, the doctor advised them that their destination required vaccinations. The doctor then injected them, not with a vaccine, but with a narcotic that allowed him to transfer them to a special killing room. The victims were never seen or heard from again, and the doctor amassed a fortune.

"The Butcher of Paris," as the doctor would become known, was actually Marcel André Henri Félix Petiot. Born January 17, 1897 in a quaint town about 100 miles (160 kilometers) southeast of Paris,

Marcel Petiot

Petiot was the elder of two children. Petiot's mother died when he was fifteen years old, but even before that, his aunt was his primary caregiver. As a boy, Petiot showed some of the classic signs of a psychopathic personality: He tortured and killed animals, including his pet kitten. He wet the bed and sometimes his pants until he was twelve years old. He was very bright, but was expelled from several schools for his misbehavior, including one time when he brought a gun to the classroom and fired it at the ceiling. He was arrested for theft, and a psychiatrist diagnosed him with mental illness in 1914.

Later, Petiot would say that he felt abandoned by his parents. The only person he was close to was his younger brother, Maurice.[16]

Petiot joined the army in 1916 and fought in World War I. During the Second Battle of Aisne, he was wounded and gassed and was sent to various hospitals and rest homes, where he was accused (and later arrested) for stealing from other patients. Army blankets, medical supplies, even wallets and photographs were snatched from the sick and dying by Petiot. In a psychiatric hospital he was diagnosed with various mental illnesses, but during times of war, it was not enough to keep him from battle. A few weeks after returning to the front, a grenade wounded him in the foot—an injury that some said was self-inflicted.

Petiot was discharged from the army with a medical pension. He went to medical school and graduated with honors in 1921. He set up a medical practice in Villeneuve-sur-Yonne, about 75 miles (120 km) southeast of Paris. His patients adored him. He worked on Sundays for those whose jobs made it hard to see him during the week. He gave discounts or even free care to elderly and poor patients. He could afford to do this because he signed his patients up for public assistance without their knowledge, and collected their money from the state.

Petiot's years in Villeneuve-sur-Yonne were marked by a series of petty thefts, bizarre behavior, and three possible murders, including that of his housekeeper and lover. After the third murder, Petiot's standing in the community became precarious. He, along with his wife and son, moved to Paris in 1933. Once again, he built a successful medical practice, but a psychiatrist who evaluated Petiot after he was caught stealing a book and threatening to assault a police officer, found him to be "deeply disturbed, unbalanced, neurotic, and 'dangerous to himself and others.'"[17]

Petiot spent a year in a mental institution. He was released in 1937, and with the exception of committing tax fraud, he stayed out of trouble for a few years.

When Germany invaded France in 1940, Petiot, ever the schemer, saw an opportunity to cash in on the plight of others. He bought an old house surrounded by a high wall, and spent months renovating it. He had a false door and peepholes installed in a soundproofed triangular room, with heavy iron rings attached to one wall. He dug a large pit beneath the floor of the garage and had a huge boiler put in the cellar. In 1941, he began luring his victims with his story of smuggling them out of the country—for a fee. Investigators believe most of them were killed in that triangular room, probably by gassing them, much as Hitler did in the death camps. Petiot covered the bodies with quicklime, which masks the smell of burning flesh, dismembered them, and fed them into his boiler.

One night in 1944, Petiot fed a few too many bodies into his boiler, and left the house on business. The fire burned out of control,

The luggage of his victims was used as evidence in Petoit's trial.

producing foul-smelling smoke that belched from the chimney for five days. The neighbors complained, and investigating police and firefighters found a ghastly sight: decomposing and burned body parts of men and women.

Investigators soon determined that the clothing, valuables, and cash found in the house belonged to Jewish victims hoping to flee the country. Petiot himself went into hiding, but was captured October 31, 1944.

At his trial, Petiot stuck with the story he was actually a patriotic hero, and that the bodies were those of the enemy or collaborators.

Nevertheless, the jury found him guilty of the murder of twenty-seven people. He probably killed many more.

Petiot was executed at the guillotine on May 25, 1946. His last words were, "Gentleman, I have one last piece of advice. Look away. This will not be pretty to see."[18]

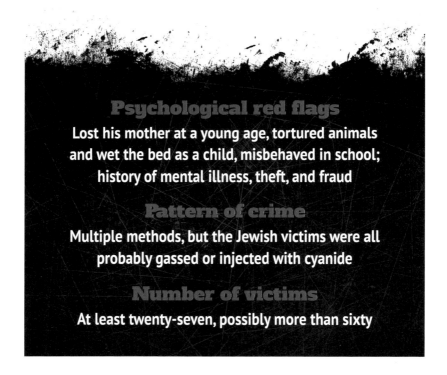

Psychological red flags

Lost his mother at a young age, tortured animals and wet the bed as a child, misbehaved in school; history of mental illness, theft, and fraud

Pattern of crime

Multiple methods, but the Jewish victims were all probably gassed or injected with cyanide

Number of victims

At least twenty-seven, possibly more than sixty

Genene Jones
aka *"The Death Nurse"*

Born: **July 13, 1950**
Occupation: **Nurse**
Motive: **Emotional gain, power**
Arrested: **November 21, 1982**

"I always cry when babies die," Genene Jones told a reporter. "You can almost explain away an adult death. When you look at an adult die, at least you can say they've had a full life. When a baby dies, they've been cheated."[19]

In fact Jones *was* known for her extreme displays of emotion upon the deaths of her tiny patients—but she was the one who cheated them out of full lives.

Genene Jones grew up in San Antonio, Texas. She was one of four adopted children. She was close to her father, Richard Jones, and loved to ride around with him as they put up billboards for his business. She would later say that those were the happiest times of her life.

Yet, with three other siblings and two working parents, Jones never felt like she got enough attention. At school, she was loud and bossy. She often pretended to be sick, just to be noticed.

Genene Jones

Jones married her high school sweetheart shortly after graduation and became a beautician. She had a baby, but their marriage was rocky, and they divorced. She would later tell people that he was abusive, a charge that she probably made up to gain sympathy. Being a beautician bored her, and so she took a one-year course to become a licensed vocational nurse (LVN).

Jones began working at the pediatric ICU at Bexar County Hospital on October 30, 1978. Her very first patient was a very ill infant who died. One of the registered nurses found it odd that Jones "went berserk," sobbing dramatically, staring at the body—even though she had spent very little time caring for the child. Jones would demonstrate this level of attention-grabbing emotion every time one of her patients died—and there would be a lot of them.

There always seemed to be a lot of drama on Jones' shifts. Babies would go into cardiac arrest, have seizures or difficulty breathing—and Jones was always there to heroically save them. Except sometimes they died anyway. Between May and November 1981, ten babies died unexpectedly under Jones' care. Hospital administrators investigated the deaths, concluding "this association of Nurse Jones with the deaths of ten children could be coincidental. However, negligence or wrong-doing cannot be excluded."[20] Fearful of bad press and the threat of a lawsuit, the hospital quietly let Jones go.

Jones quickly found a new job at a new pediatric clinic nearby run by a young doctor, Kathy Holland. Holland had worked with Jones as a resident at the hospital. She liked the nurse and respected her skills. She dismissed the rumors about Jones as so much gossip.

Medical Serial Killers

The same pattern soon emerged at the clinic—a baby would go into some kind of crisis, and Jones would be there save the day. One of her first patients was fifteen-month-old Chelsea McClellan, who had a case of the sniffles. While the doctor was talking with the child's mother, Jones took care of the baby in the examining room. Suddenly, Jones screamed that the baby stopped breathing. She cared for the baby heroically in the ambulance on the way to the hospital, and the baby pulled through. A few weeks later, Chelsea returned for a follow-up exam. This time, the little girl stopped breathing and went into a seizure after Jones gave her an injection. She died before reaching the hospital. A little boy suffered a seizure and went into respiratory arrest that same day. He recovered, but Jones was reportedly very excited about the drama.

An investigation into these incidents and those at the hospital revealed that Jones had injected the children with life-threatening drugs, and then tried to save them so that she could be the hero.

Jones was found guilty of one count of murder, and one count of attempted murder. Investigators believe she may have killed as many as forty-seven children. She was sentenced to life in prison. Unless investigators can prove she killed more children, she will be released in 2018.

Jones is suspected of poisoning and killing dozens of infants and children.

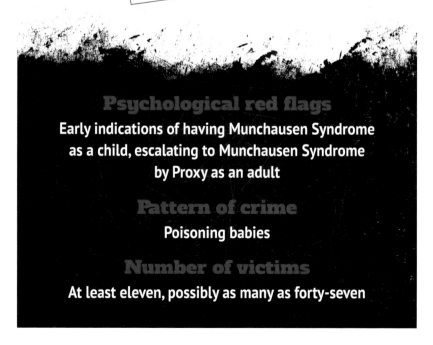

Psychological red flags

Early indications of having Munchausen Syndrome as a child, escalating to Munchausen Syndrome by Proxy as an adult

Pattern of crime

Poisoning babies

Number of victims

At least eleven, possibly as many as forty-seven

Richard Angelo
aka "The Long Island Angel of Death"

Born: **April 29, 1962**

Occupation: **Nurse**

Motive: **Emotional gain**

Arrested: **October 12, 1987**

Richard Angelo loved playing the hero. In a taped confession, he said "I wanted to create a situation where I would cause the patient to have some respiratory distress or some problems, and through my intervention or suggested intervention or whatever, come out looking like I knew what I was doing. I had no confidence in myself. I felt very inadequate."[21]

If Angelo had more confidence in himself—less of a need to be a hero—he might well have been an admirable man, if not a true hero. Born in Lindenhurst, New Jersey, he was the only child of a high school guidance counselor and a home economics teacher. He was an Eagle Scout as a teenager, and later, a volunteer fireman and a volunteer emergency medical technician (EMT). He seemed a quiet, unassuming young man. A neighbor said, "The family was a nice family and the boy was a nice boy, but very few people knew them well enough."[22]

Angelo earned a degree in nursing in 1985. Again, he kept a low profile; his professors said he did not stand out. He landed a job

Richard Angelo

when he was twenty-six years old at the Good Samaritan Hospital in West Islip, Long Island, in April 1987. As the low man on the totem pole, he was assigned the graveyard shift—11 p.m. to 7 a.m.—in the cardiac and ICU.

Like many health care serial killers, this lonely shift suited Angelo just fine. It would be easier to slip into a hospital room, inject a drug into the patient's IV line, and then return moments later to play the hero. In his first attempt, he miscalculated the drug's potency, and he was unable to revive his patient. Undeterred, Angelo decided that he just needed to refine his technique. In September and October of 1987, Angelo created thirty-seven life-threatening emergencies. He was able to revive just twelve of his victims.

On October 11, Gerolamo Kucich saw a man inject something into his IV line. As he felt himself slipping into unconsciousness, he managed to press his call button. A nurse responding to his call—not Angelo—managed to revive him. When he was able to speak, he described the incident. Kucich's nurse sent his urine sample in for analysis. What they found was evidence of attempted murder: The sample tested positive for two paralyzing drugs that had not been prescribed for the patient.

The next day, police searched Angelo's locker and home. Sure enough, they found vials of both drugs. They arrested Angelo, who confessed to the murder of several people. The bodies of his suspected victims were exhumed and tested for the drugs; all were positive.

Angelo's lawyers made the argument that their client suffered from dissociative identity disorder. This meant that he had multiple

Richard Angelo appears in court on October 4, 1989, in
Riverhead, New York.

personalities that he could move in and out of, each unaware of the actions of the other personality.

Ultimately, Angelo was convicted of two counts of second-degree murder, one count of second-degree manslaughter, one count of criminally negligent homicide, and six counts of assault. He was sentenced to sixty-one years to life in prison.[23]

Psychological red flags
Severe lack of self-esteem

Pattern of crime
Poisoning men and women

Number of victims
At least twenty-five

Beverly Allitt

Born: October 4, 1968
Occupation: Nurse
Motive: Emotional gain
Arrested: November 1991

As a child, Beverly Allitt showed all the signs of having Munchausen's Syndrome, a condition that would continue into adulthood. But as a newly minted nurse, her attention-seeking behavior took a deadlier turn: She found that she could attract even more attention by killing her young patients.

Allitt, one of four children, was born and raised in the village of Corby Glen, England. She seemed to have a fairly normal childhood, although she often insisted on wearing bandages over "wounds" that she would never reveal. Her need for attention grew as she entered adolescence and she began to struggle with her weight. She was constantly complaining of stomach cramps, headaches, backaches or vomiting. She frequently "accidentally" cut herself with a knife or had some other injury. Crutches and arm slings were a common sight on Allitt. She lied to her boyfriends and was verbally and physically abusive.

Allitt left school when she was sixteen to enter a prenursing program at nearby Grantham College, where her medical complaints escalated. She even convinced surgeons to remove her appendix—which turned out to be perfectly fine. She was suspected of smearing feces on the walls in a nursing home where she did her training.

Given her record, it was not surprising that Grantham Hospital, in Lincolnshire England, initially turned twenty-three-year-old Beverly Allitt down for a job. Although she had passed her written nursing exams, she had taken so much sick leave that she lacked the necessary number of hours on the floor. But they were desperately short-staffed, and hired her on a six-month contract to work on the children's ward.

Allitt claimed her first victim in February 1991, the same week she began working at Grantham Hospital. One of her first patients was Liam Taylor, a baby whose bad cold threatened to turn into pneumonia. The little boy had two cardiac arrests—extremely rare in babies. The second one caused severe brain damage, and he died. As with all of her murders, she would show a great deal of excitement and concern during the crisis—and then appear emotionally flat after the deaths of her victims.

Two weeks later, an eleven-year-old boy with cerebral palsy died of cardiac arrest under Allitt's watch, followed by a two-month-old premature twin girl. Such was Allitt's charm that the girl's parents named her as the godmother of the surviving twin. There were a number of other close calls after that. By now the staff at Grantham Hospital knew something was seriously wrong. Was there some sort of virus going around? A tainted batch of some drug? There was even talk of a Munchausen Syndrome by Proxy killer, and whispers about Allitt, but nobody followed through.

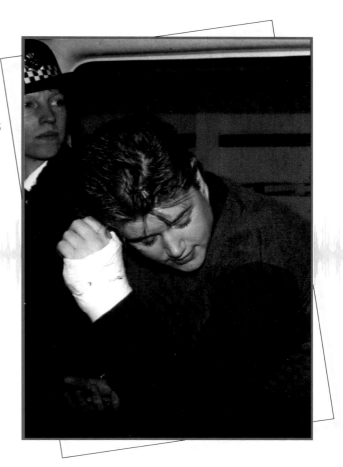

Beverly Allitt arrives at the Grantham Magistrate's court on December 19, 1991.

The death of Claire Peck, a fifteen-month-old asthmatic child, finally prompted an inquiry. Once again, she had died of a heart attack under Allitt's care. Doctors examining her body found high levels of a drug normally used in cardiac arrest, but never in a baby.

Investigators examined the many suspicious deaths in the ward, and found one common factor: Beverly Allitt was involved in every instance. They determined that she had killed her patients by injecting them with insulin or sometimes, simply bubbles of air.

She was charged with four counts of murder, eleven counts of attempted murder, and eleven counts of causing grievous bodily harm.

Allitt was arrested and released on bail. While she was out on bail, she attempted to kill her goddaughter, the surviving twin. She did not succeed, but the girl had permanent brain damage. After she was arrested a second time in September 1991, she began to starve herself. The prison authorities were baffled when she began to vomit. What was coming up? They found she was swallowing her own feces—a continuing symptom of Munchausen's Syndrome.

On May 23, 1993, Allitt was convicted and given thirteen life sentences for murder and attempted murder.[24]

Psychological red flags
Childhood symptoms of Munchausen's Syndrome, escalating to Munchausen Syndrome by Proxy as an adult

Pattern of crime
Poisoning babies

Number of victims
Four

Chapter 3

THE LUST- AND THRILL-ORIENTED HEDONISTS

Lust killers and thrill killers share a common motivation: sex. Both types of killers have somehow made a personal connection between killing and sexual gratification.[1] For lust killers, sex is an integral part of the act of killing and often after the victim is dead. Thrill killers, on the other hand, may get a sexual rush from the act of killing, but it is not directed toward the victim. Once their victims are dead, thrill killers lose all interest in the body, although they often take personal items as "trophies."

Jane Toppan

aka "Jolly Jane"

Born: **1854–1857**

Occupation: **Nurse**

Motive: **Lust**

Arrested: **October 29, 1901**

Died: **August 17, 1938**

Jane Toppan is one of the few female serial lust-driven killers. Her motive, she confessed, was "the desire to experience sexual excitement by killing people."[2] Murder, she said, gave her the "greatest conceivable pleasure."[3]

Jane Toppan was born Honora Kelly, the youngest of four sisters in a poor family of Irish immigrants in Massachusetts. Her mother died when she was just a year old. Her father, a tailor named Peter Kelly, sank into severe alcoholism and mental illness. Legend has it that later in life he tried to sew his eyelids shut. In 1863, he brought six-year-old Honora and her eight-year-old sister Delia to an orphanage for girls. It is not known whether Kelly abused his daughters, but they were clearly neglected.

Ann Toppan, of Lowell, Massachusetts, took Honora in as a kind of indentured servant when the girl was eight years old. The Toppans never formally adopted Honora, but she took the family name and became known as Jane Toppan.

Jane Toppan

ood feelings of shame and self-loathing ar
sychopaths. In the middle-class Protestant soci
habited, it was humiliating to be Irish. Italian i
ly higher up on the ladder of social respectabili
her thick dark hair, olive skin, prominent nose
was passed off as an Italian orphan whose p
. In private, Mrs. Toppan never failed to remind t
e made her socially inferior. Jane internalized th
making derogatory remarks about the Irish and

Jane compensated for her feelings of inferiority by becoming the life of the party. She had the psychopath's charm that made her popular among many of her schoolmates, and she told wild stories about her family: Her father had sailed around the world and lived in China; her beautiful sister had married an English lord; and President Lincoln had given her brother a medal for his heroism at Gettysburg.[4]

Mrs. Toppan was a strict disciplinarian, and always made sure that Jane knew her place in the household. By all accounts Jane's foster sister Elizabeth treated her with kindness and respect, but Jane envied her privilege. When Mrs. Toppan died, Elizabeth inherited the family house. Jane got nothing. She stayed on at the house as a servant, quietly seething. Jane moved out shortly after Elizabeth married a church deacon, Oramel Brigham. She was around thirty-one years old at the time. With no husband or prospect of marriage, she needed to provide for herself, and so in 1887 she began nurse's training at Boston's Cambridge Hospital.

Toppan's habit of gossiping, spreading rumors, and stealing did not endear her to her fellow students and supervisors. But like many psychopaths, she was able to present an entirely different face to senior staff and patients. They called her "Jolly Jane."

Jane devised ways of keeping those patients she liked in the hospital longer. She made them sicker by giving them small doses of poison, or falsified their charts. Those she did not like were the subjects of her "scientific experiments." At first, she gave her patients morphine, watching her patients as they slipped into a deep sleep. With a large-enough dose, they fell into a coma and died. She found that it was much more exciting to follow up the morphine

The old nurses' building in Cambridge Hospital from the late nineteenth century, when Toppan worked there.

with atropine, which induced a kind of giddy delirium, spasms, and convulsions. Occasionally, she would wait until her victim was near death and then heroically pull them back from the brink. Investigators speculated that she killed more than a dozen patients while working at Cambridge Hospital.

In 1888, Jane transferred to the more reputable Massachusetts General Hospital for further training. She continued her "experiments" there and claimed several more victims. One patient who survived Jolly Jane's experiment would later describe how the nurse had given her some sort of medication that sent her into a semi-conscious state. The patient remembered Toppan climbing into bed with her. The nurse caressed the patient and stroked her hair. The patient resisted taking the dose of medicine Toppan tried to force on her. A disturbance outside the room caused Jolly Jane to leave; it may well have saved the patient's life.

Toppan became a private nurse after being dismissed from the hospital for being careless with drugs and stealing. Such was her charm that she became one of the most successful private nurses in Cambridge, even though she was known to lie and steal. Her murders took on a more personal character. She killed her elderly landlord, and two years later his wife, because they had become "'feeble and fussy' and 'old and cranky.'"[5]

In 1899, Toppan invited her foster sister Elizabeth to join her at a cottage she was renting on Cape Cod. Two days after her arrival, Elizabeth's husband, Oramel Brigham, received an urgent telegram: Elizabeth had fallen seriously ill. She died the next day, apparently of a stroke. Years later, Toppan would say that she wanted revenge on Elizabeth. She deliberately prolonged her foster sister's death, she said, cuddling and fondling her as she died.[6]

Next, she targeted the family who owned the Cape Cod home she rented. The mother, Mattie Davis, was the first to go. The heartbroken family invited Toppan into their home to do some housekeeping. Toppan killed three other members of the family. A young woman named Minnie was the family's last victim, and she held Minnie's ten-year-old son in her arms as Minnie died. Toppan returned to Cambridge, where she poisoned Oramel Brigham's sister, hoping that she could get her old rival Elizabeth's husband all to herself.

Surviving members of the Davis family were convinced that Jane was somehow responsible for the deaths. They had the bodies exhumed, and found lethal levels of morphine and atropine in all of them.

Jane Toppan was arrested for the deaths of the Davis family, as well as Oramel Brigham's sister. Toppan confessed to murdering thirty-one people that she could remember, plus many others she could not recall, perhaps as many as 100.

Toppan was found not guilty by reason of insanity, and spent the remaining years of her life in a mental institution. Her mental state slowly deteriorated until her death at the age of eighty or eighty-one.

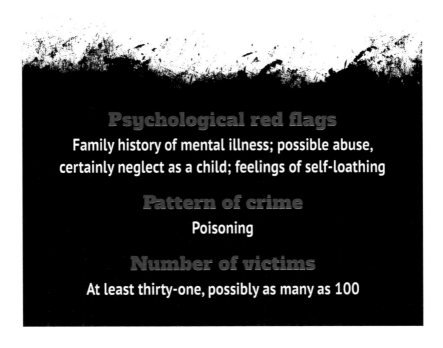

Psychological red flags

Family history of mental illness; possible abuse, certainly neglect as a child; feelings of self-loathing

Pattern of crime

Poisoning

Number of victims

At least thirty-one, possibly as many as 100

Gwendolyn Graham and Catherine Wood

aka "The Lethal Lovers"

Born: August 6, 1963 (Graham) and
July 3, 1962 (Wood)
Occupations: Nurse's aides
Motives: Thrill
Arrested: December, 1988

> *When you're mine*
> *Oh please say*
> *You'll be mine*
> *Forever and five days.*

Catherine Wood wrote those lines for her girlfriend, Gwendolyn Graham. The two of them were nurses' aides at the Alpine Manor nursing home in Walker, Michigan. The poem reflected the pledge the women made to be together forever, plus the number of days that corresponded to the number of patients they murdered.[7]

Wood was the oldest of three children. Her father drank heavily and beat her; her mother was distant and cold. Needy and lonely, she married Ken Wood at the age of seventeen, and had a bab

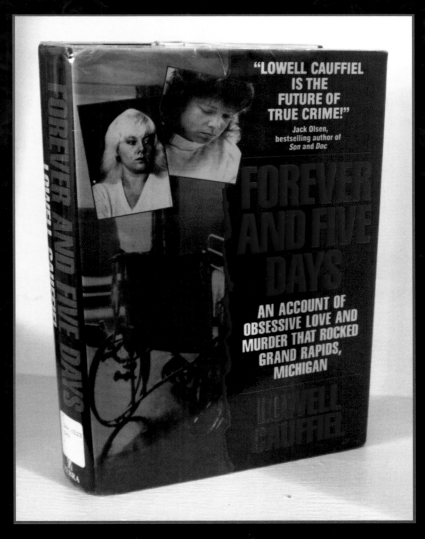

The story of Wood and Graham became a best-selling true crime narrative. It was almost stranger than fiction.

soon after. She fed her unhappiness with food, and her weight ballooned to nearly 450 pounds (204 kilograms). In 1986, she took a job as a nurses' aide at Alpine Manor, lost weight, dyed her hair platinum blonde, and had a brief affair with a colleague. Wood was soon promoted to supervisor. With a newfound sense of power, she intimidated unruly patients with her large size, take-no-prisoners attitude, and sometimes rough behavior.[8]

Graham, also the eldest of three children, had a difficult childhood as well. Her parents ignored the babies' cries, thinking it would toughen them up. Both parents were physically abusive. The teenage Graham burned herself with lit cigarettes to ease the emotional pain stemming from her father's sexual abuse. When she was seventeen, she moved in with a female lover. When her lover took a job in Grand Rapids, Graham followed her and got a job at Alpine Manor. Shortly after their relationship fell apart, Graham began an affair with Wood—an affair that would lead Wood to ask for a divorce.[9]

According to Wood (Graham disputes her story), Graham said that thinking about murder excited her sexually. In January of 1987, Graham came up with the idea of the MURDER game. They would select their victims so that the first initial of their names would read "murder." Their first victim, an Alzheimer's patient, was Marguerite Chambers. Gwen smothered the woman with a washcloth placed over the women's mouth, while Wood kept watch at the door. It soon became too difficult to target victims with appropriate names, so they began murdering those patients who were easiest to kill. In the coming months, they would kill five patients, with Graham doing the suffocating and Wood playing lookout. Immediately after, the women would hurry to an empty room and make love, excited by their murderous acts. They took personal items from their victims as keepsakes.

Graham began to pressure Wood to take a more active role in the killings, but Wood refused. This angered Graham, who began an affair with another woman.

Graham and her new lover moved to Texas in April 1987, but she wrote disturbing letters to Wood, describing how she wanted to smash the faces of the babies in her care. Alarmed, Wood confessed everything to her ex-husband, who eventually told the police.

Although investigators could find no physical evidence that the five victims had in fact been murdered, Cathy Wood pleaded guilty to second degree murder and conspiracy to commit murder, in exchange for testifying against Gwen Graham. Graham claimed that the patients had all died from normal causes, and that Wood had made up the story to get back at her for breaking off their relationship. But Wood's testimony, and the fact that Graham had told her new girlfriend that she had killed six patients, was damning evidence. Wood was sentenced to twenty to forty years in prison. Graham was given six life sentences at Huron Valley Women's Correctional Facility in Michigan, with no possibility of parole.

Huron Valley Women's Correctional Facility

Psychological red flags
Both women were psychologically needy,
the victims of childhood abuse

Pattern of crime
Smothering elderly female patients

Number of victims
Five

Michael Swango
aka "Double-O Swango"

Born: October 21, 1954
Occupation: Physician
Motive: Thrill
Arrested: June, 1997

Michael Swango's classmates gave him the nickname "Double-O Swango" because, like James Bond (007), it appeared that he had a license to kill. His patients had a way of getting even sicker or even dying. Little did they know that their joking nickname was very close to the truth.

Michael's father, Virgil, was a career army officer, and so most of his childhood was spent moving from one army base to another. The family finally settled in Quincy, Illinois, when Michael was thirteen years old. Virgil Swango was a heavy drinker, and Michael's parents separated. Michael's older brother Robert described their family life as "emotionally starved."[10]

Michael was exceptionally bright. He breezed through high school, graduating as the valedictorian of his class. A gifted musician and track star, he was popular, and voted "most likely to succeed."

Michael went to college in a nearby town on a music scholarship and did well for two years. His life took a turn when his girlfriend

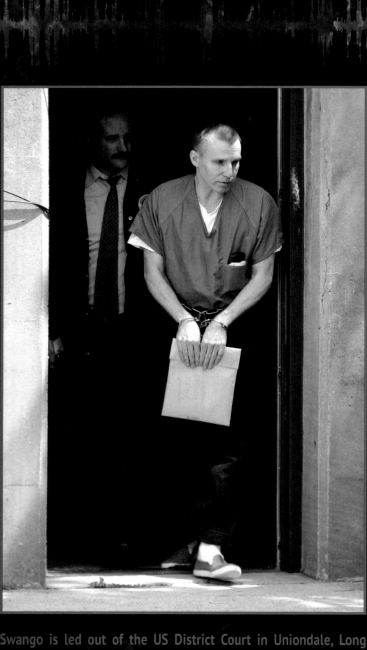

Swango is led out of the US District Court in Uniondale, Long Island, New York, after pleading not guilty in 2000.

broke up with him. Swango dropped out of college and joined the Marines as a medic. He became fascinated with violence of all sorts, and filled scrapbooks with newspaper clippings about car accidents, mass murders, and serial killers. Given an honorable discharge in 1976, he returned to college with a goal: to get into medical school and become a doctor.

He finished college with high grades, but his experience in medical school was spotty at best: he had few friends, frequently cheated on exams, botched his cadaver dissections, and had such a sloppy attitude toward his patients in his clinical rotations that some of his fellow students tried to get him kicked out of medical school. Swango had the psychopath's trademark charm, however, and managed to convince the school's administrators to keep him on, even though he failed a rotation and had to repeat it.

Despite his dismal grades and poor letters of recommendation, Swango was accepted for an internship at Ohio State University Medical Center. Hospital nurses began to notice that there were an alarming number of deaths and medical crises when Swango was on the floor. The nurses reported their suspicions to hospital administrators, who dismissed them as mere gossip.

Swango was not hired as a resident after his internship—not because he was suspected of murder, but because he did sloppy work. Hospital administrators agreed to give Swango a letter of reference and did not report his poor performance to the authorities.

Swango returned to Quincy in the summer of 1984. He got a job as an EMT and began to experiment with poisoning his colleagues. When it became clear that he had laced his colleagues' pizza with rat poison, Swango was convicted of aggravated battery and sentenced to five years in prison. In 1987, he was released for good behavior after serving only thirty months.

After a series of odd jobs, Swango found his way back into medicine by changing his name to Daniel J. Adams and forging documents, including a document stating that his legal record from Illinois was about a fist fight, (a misdemeanor), rather than attempted murder (a felony).

During this time, he met Kristen Kinney, a registered nurse at Riverside Hospital in Newport news, Virginia. The two fell in love and planned to marry. Kinney began having persistent headaches, which miraculously ended after the couple separated in 1992.

He landed a job in July 1992 at the Sanford USD Medical Center in Souix Falls, South Dakota, but left soon after. He moved from one hospital to another as administrators learned of his true identity and history, leaving a trail of mysterious deaths behind him.

Swango fled the country in 1993, emerging at last in Zimbabwe. He was readily hired at a remote mission hospital, where the killings soon resumed. He was arrested and charged with five murders, but he left the country before he could be brought to trial. He hopped from one hospital to another in Africa. He had to pass through a Chicago airport in 1997, and there US authorities arrested him.

At his trial, prosecutors read passages from his journal, in which Swango wrote of his pleasure at poisoning people in hospitals. A fatal bus accident involving children was one of his favorite fantasies, and he loved coming out of the emergency room (ER) to tell parents that their child was dead. Although Swango maintained that he was not guilty, he pled guilty to three murders in New York in order to escape the death penalty and possible extradition to

An assistant US attorney shows the media a page from Swango's journal.

Zimbabwe. Swango's true number of victims is probably somewhere between thirty-five and sixty. He is currently serving three consecutive life terms in prison.

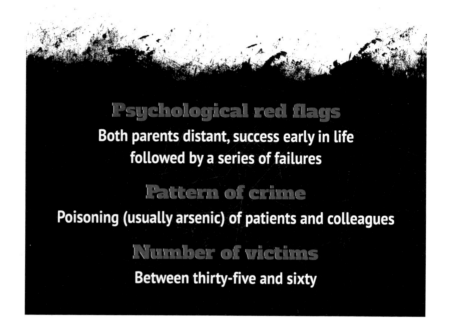

Psychological red flags
Both parents distant, success early in life followed by a series of failures

Pattern of crime
Poisoning (usually arsenic) of patients and colleagues

Number of victims
Between thirty-five and sixty

Chapter 4

THE TREATMENT
SERIAL KILLERS

It is not immediately obvious that treatment killer doctors intend for their patients to die. Some suffer from mental or physical impairments that cause them to make deadly mistakes—over and over again. If this type of treatment killer has a great deal of authority or charisma, it can be difficult for those with less power to force him or her to step down. Other treatment killers have such grandiose ideas of themselves and their often-unconventional treatments that they accept patient deaths as a necessary risk. They refuse to acknowledge that their "treatments" may very well cause death.[1]

Linda Burfield Hazzard

Born: **1868**
Occupation: **Physician, "fasting specialist"**
Motive: **Treatment killing, gain**
Arrested: **August 1911**
Died: **1938**

In her book *Fasting for the Cure of Disease,* the self-proclaimed "fasting specialist" Linda Burfield Hazzard wrote "... eating has long pandered to the sense of taste, and appetite is cultivated at the expense of digestion.... Overeating is a well-nigh universal vice...."[2] She convinced her wealthy patients that starvation was the key to curing disease.

Linda Burfield was born in western Minnesota, the eldest of seven children. She was an athletic, outgoing child. Her parents ate a mostly vegetarian diet, which was unusual for a farm family at that time. A doctor convinced the parents that the children, who were quite healthy, had potentially fatal intestinal parasites. He prescribed blue pills as treatment, which caused terrible vomiting and diarrhea. Incredibly, this happened year after year. The young woman was convinced that these "treatments" damaged her digestive system, and vowed to search for a cure.[3]

Burfield married Erwin Perry at the age of eighteen and had two children, but she soon divorced her husband and shipped her children

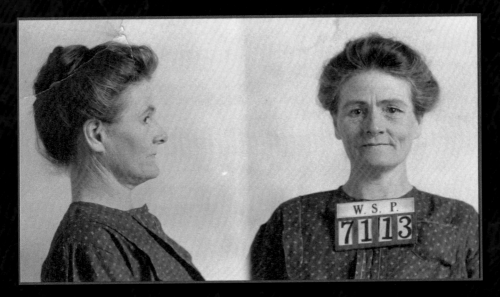

Hazzard had wanted to revolutionize medicine. Instead, she starved her patients to death.

off to live with their grandmother. She had greater ambitions than motherhood: She wanted to revolutionize medicine. She moved to Minneapolis, where she hit upon the idea of fasting as a way of curing just about any disease, from a toothache to tuberculosis. She thought that periodic fasting allowed the digestive system to rest and be cleansed of toxins. One of her patients died of starvation around 1902 (somehow "losing" her valuable rings in the process), but she was never prosecuted.

In 1906, she moved to Seattle, Washington with her second husband, Samuel Hazzard. She studied osteopathic medicine—a kind of alternative medicine that emphasizes the treatment of medical disorders through the manipulation of the body's muscle tissue and bones—and was licensed by the state as a "fasting specialist." She set up a sanitarium outside of the nearby town of Olalla, naming it Wilderness Heights. Locals would soon come to call it "Starvation Heights."[4]

Visitors to her sanitarium consumed only small servings of tomato or asparagus broth for weeks. They received daily enemas that lasted for hours, and vigorous, painful massages. Not surprisingly, several of Hazzard's patients died. Hazzard insisted they were already at death's door when they arrived.

In late February 1911, two wealthy British sisters, Claire and Dora Williamson, came to Seattle for the "starvation cure." Two months later, the sisters were so weak and emaciated they could hardly move. Weighing just 70 pounds (31 kg) each, they were transferred to Wilderness Heights on stretchers. Claire managed to persuade a worker on the grounds to send a telegram to their childhood nanny, Margaret Conway. By the time Conway arrived, Claire had died. Dora, who was down to 50 pounds (22 kg) and delirious from starvation, had to be persuaded to leave.

Conway learned that Hazzard had been appointed the executor of Claire's estate, as well as Dora's guardian for life. She—or whoever wrote Claire's last wishes—stipulated that her valuable jewelry should go to Hazzard and her nurses.

Conway suspected that Claire had been starved to death intentionally—she was murdered for her money. Investigators

This man was fasting for a cure, as per Hazzard's orders. It was taken the fiftieth day of his fast, and he weighed just 105 lbs (47 kg).

determined that a least a dozen people lost their lives and much of their money under Hazzard's care. Dora survived, and when Hazzard was brought to trial, testified against her. Hazzard was found guilty of manslaughter and served two years in prison. When she got out, she resumed her business, starving still more people to death.

Hazzard died in 1938, when she succumbed to her own starvation treatment.

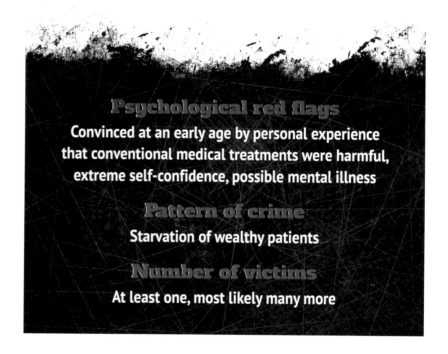

Psychological red flags
Convinced at an early age by personal experience that conventional medical treatments were harmful, extreme self-confidence, possible mental illness

Pattern of crime
Starvation of wealthy patients

Number of victims
At least one, most likely many more

Harry Bailey

Born: 1922
Occupation: Psychiatrist, "deep-sleep therapist"
Method: Treatment killing
Arrested: Committed suicide before arrest
Died: September 8, 1985

Harry Bailey, like other treatment killers, may have truly believed that his unorthodox therapies really worked. Still, when the "cure" kills patient after patient, most reasonable people would admit that they were wrong, and turn to treatments that actually work. Not Harry Bailey, the "deep-sleep therapist."

Bailey was born in New South Wales, Australia. Educational opportunities for a bright boy like Bailey were limited in that part of Australia, so his working-class family sent him to a boarding school in Sydney. His younger brother and sister, who did not get such preferential treatment, were in awe of him.[5]

Always a self-promoter, it appears that he later tried to give the impression that he attended a much more prestigious school than the one he actually attended. He attended medical school in Sydney, and throughout his career never failed to point out that he won a prize awarded to the best psychiatry student. He always forgot to

Psychiatrist Harry Bailey appears at the Court of Petty Sessions, Sydney, Australia, November 7, 1984.

mention that there were only three students competing for the prize. He went on to specialize in psychiatry. His wife Marjorie, who he married while in medical school, said that psychiatry appealed to him because he would not have to work long hours. Perhaps as important, the specialty was not popular at the time, so it was a wide-open field for a self-promoter like Bailey to make a name for himself.[6]

After medical school, Bailey dabbled in various faddish cures for mental illness, including taking part in an experiment in which he took hallucinogenic drugs. He went into private practice and became quite wealthy as a result of his high fees and fraudulent Medicare and private insurance claims.

In 1963, Bailey set up a deep-sleep therapy (DST) ward in the Chelmsford Hospital in Sydney. The therapy stems from the belief that if people could be induced to sleep during an emotional crisis, the brain would sort things out and all would be well when they awakened. There was little scientific evidence to support the theory.

Bailey would give his patients barbituates, often without explaining their purpose, to put them into comas that could last as long as a month. During the comas, he sometimes administered electroconvulsive therapy (ECT).

Many of his DST patients died of pneumonia or by choking on their own vomit. Fifteen of the documented twenty-six deaths related to DST were suicides that occurred after the treatment. As the deaths mounted, Bailey's practices were coming under intense scrutiny. Doctors stopped referring patients to Bailey, and his practice became a scandal. Facing numerous legal charges, Bailey took an overdose of sleeping pills and washed them down with a beer.

Dr. Harry Bailey gives a speech at the Mentally Retarded Conference in Ryde, Australia, September 15, 1961.

He wrote a suicide note in which he portrayed himself as a "martyr to scientific progress."[7]

A former student of Bailey's portrayed him somewhat differently: "He was an incredibly bright fellow—there was no question at all about his intelligence, it was way out. But my view is that he was a psychopath in the sense of somebody who had a very faulty conscience. He regarded himself as a superior person. Sometimes he managed to cover that up a little bit but he could never hide it for that long. He could get away with all sorts of things without any obvious feelings of guilt that you or I would feel."[8]

Psychological red flags

Extreme self-promotion and exaggeration

Pattern of crime

Inducing comas with barbituates, resulting in death from pneumonia, stroke, or heart attack, or subsequent suicides

Number of victims

At least twenty-six

Ferdinand Sauerbruch

Born: July 3, 1875
Occupation: Surgeon
Motive: Treatment killing
Arrested: Not arrested or convicted
Died: July 2, 1951

Ferdinand Sauerbruch, a German doctor, was one of the most celebrated surgeons of the twentieth century. He designed a pressure chamber that allowed surgeons to perform surgery on the lungs, heart, and esophagus. As a battlefield surgeon in World War I, he developed several new types of limb prostheses. He invented the strategy, now routinely used by surgeons everywhere, of rehearsing difficult operations ahead of time.

His reputation was such that the rich and famous sought him out, yet he would waive his fees if his patients were poor.[9] Although he received an award from the Nazi party, he disliked Hitler and privately supported victims of the Nazis.[10]

And yet there was another side to Sauerbruch, one that would lead to his tragic downfall and the deaths of many patients.

Sauerbruch's origins were humble. Born in Barmen, Germany, his father died of tuberculosis when he was just two years old. His grandfather became his legal guardian, and by his own accounts, his childhood had "more bitterness and frustration than happiness."[11]

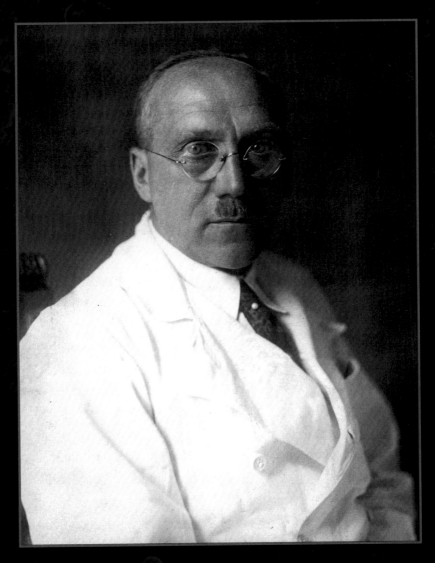

Ferdinand Sauerbruch

When World War II broke out in 1939, Sauerbruch was head of the Charité Hospital in Berlin. Sauerbruch was supremely confident in his own abilities, and was intolerant of anyone who did not live up to his high standards. He could be abusive in the operating room, lashing out at any little lapse among his staff. Yet he was greatly admired for his dedication to his patients and his great skill as a surgeon. He was so famous and skilled that he was called to operate on Mussolini, Lenin, and the king of Greece.

After the war ended, Sauerbruch developed hardening of the arteries of the brain, a condition that leads to dementia. Colleagues noticed that the once-brilliant surgeon was becoming increasingly confused. He would get lost and wander about in bewilderment. Worse, his behavior began to affect his work. He physically assaulted a fellow surgeon who pointed out that he was operating with dirty hands. One time, he rushed into a surgery where a patient was being operated on for a brain tumor. He pulled the tumor out with his bare hands and waved it about, saying "Look! They think they are surgeons! I went right in and pulled it out. The finger is still the surgeon's best instrument." The patient died two days later.[12]

There were other complaints from hospital staff, but the hospital administrators, eager to profit from Sauerbruch's prestige, refused to bar the doctor from surgery. Sauerbruch's condition worsened, and although the staff tried to keep him away from patients, they didn't always succeed. Still confident in his skills as surgeon, he bungled one surgery after another. Sauerbruch was finally forced to retire in 1949.

Even then, patients flocked to the famous doctor's home. He performed operations without anesthetic on his dining room table,

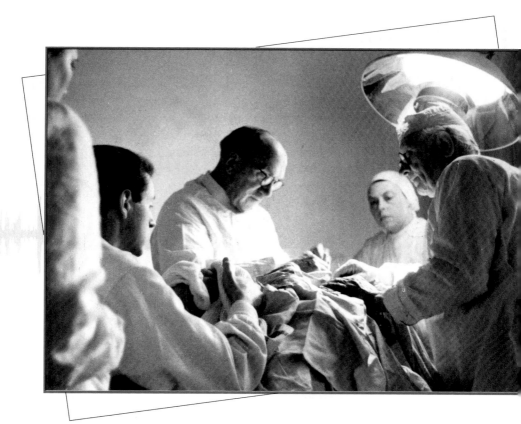

Sauerbruch held himself and everyone around him to impossibly high standards.

using needles and thread from his wife's sewing kit. Neighbors complained about the screams, but nothing could be done. His wife tried to prevent him from seeing patients, but he was determined— and so were the patients, convinced that the surgeon was still great.

According to forensic psychiatrist Robert Kaplan, Sauerbruch killed "scores" of patients before dying of a brain hemorrhage in 1951, at the age of seventy-four.[13]

Psychological red flags

Exaggerated sense of competence; dementia

Pattern of crime

Botched surgeries due to dementia

Number of victims

Unknown

Chapter 4

CONCLUSION

There is no generic profile that can describe a medical serial killer. There are certain traits, however, that are common among serial killers: the need for control, predatory behavior, disregard for the law, sensation seeking, and a lack of empathy, remorse, or guilt. These traits and behaviors all fit within the psychopathic personality disorder.

The question of whether psychopathic serial killers can be rehabilitated is a controversial one. A recent study using magnetic resonance imaging (MRI) brain scans of psychopathic violent criminals suggests that rehabilitation is not likely to work. Compared with the brains of nonpsychopathic criminals and healthy noncriminals, the psychopathic criminals had abnormalities in the brain regions associated with learning from reward and punishment. Most people make decisions based on the positive and negative consequences of their actions, choosing the action most likely to lead to a positive outcome. Psychopaths may consider only the possible positive consequences of their actions, failing to take account of the negatives.[1]

While adult psychopaths may be beyond rehabilitation, the authors of the study believe that it might be possible to alter the brain structure and function of children with psychopathic tendencies. "Since most violent crimes are committed by men who display conduct problems from a young age, learning-based interventions that target the specific brain mechanisms underlying the behavior pattern and thereby change the behavior would significantly reduce violent crime," Sheilagh Hodgins, one of the authors of the paper told *LiveScience*.[2]

At the very least, it would seem that those health care serial killers who have been released from prison should never, ever go near a medical facility—except as patients. And while there may be no way of preventing serial killers from entering health care professions, improved personnel screening, record-keeping, and other safeguards may catch them earlier.

Psychopathy Quiz

Are You a Psychopath?

This quiz is designed to help give you some insight into people with psychopathic tendencies. While the quiz is not meant to diagnose psychopathy, it may also give you an idea about whether or not *you* have such tendencies.

Read each of the following statements and answer each honestly. Give yourself two points if the statement definitely describes you, one point if it somewhat describes you, and zero points if it doesn't describe you at all. Tally up the points to see where *you* sit on the psychopathy scale!

1. I'd rather be spontaneous than make plans.
2. I wouldn't have a problem cheating on a boyfriend or girlfriend if I knew I could get away with it.
3. I don't mind ditching plans to hang out with my friends if something better comes along—like a chance to go out with that hot new guy or girl.
4. Seeing animals injured or in pain doesn't bother me.
5. I love excitement and danger.
6. I think it's OK to manipulate others so that I can get ahead.
7. I'm a smooth talker: I can always get people to do what I want them to do.
8. I'm great at making quick decisions.
9. I don't get it when movies or TV shows make people cry.

10. Most people just bring problems upon themselves, so why should I help them?

11. I'm rarely to blame when things go wrong—it's others who are incompetent, not me.

12. I have more talent in the tip of my little finger than most people will ever have.

13. I am able to make other people believe my lies.

14. I don't feel guilty when I make people feel bad.

15. I often borrow things and then lose or forget to return them.

16. I skip school or work more than most people I know.

17. I tend to blurt out exactly what's on my mind.

18. I often get into trouble because I lie a lot.

19. I skip school and/or often don't get my assignments done on time.

20. I think that crying is a sign of weakness.

If you scored 30–40 points, you have many psychopath tendencies.

If you scored 20–39 points, you have some psychopathic tendencies.

If you scored 0–19 points, you have no psychopathic tendencies.

Chapter Notes

Introduction

1. Robert M. Kaplan, *Medical Murder: Disturbing Cases of Doctors Who Kill* (Sydney, Australia: Allen & Unwin, 2009), p. 50 (large print version).
2. Herbert G. Kinnell, "Serial Homicide by Doctors: Shipman in Perspective," *British Medical Journal* 321, no. 23-20 (December 2000): 1594–1597.
3. Katherine Ramsland, *Inside the Minds of Healthcare Serial Killers: Why They Kill* (Westport, CT: Praeger, 2007), p. xii.
4. Robert J. Morton and Mark A. Hilts, eds., "Serial Murder: Multidisciplinary Perspectives for Investigators," Behavioral Analysis Unit, National Center for the Analysis of Violent Crime, Federal Bureau of Investigation, 2005, http://www.fbi.gov/stats-services/publications/serial-murder (accessed May 11, 2015).
5. Robert Kaplan, "The Clinicide Phenomenon: An Exploration of Medical Murder," *Australasian Psychiatry* 15, no. 4 (August 2007): 299–304.

Chapter 1: The Power Seekers

1. Katherine Ramsland, *Inside the Minds of Healthcare Serial Killers: Why They Kill* (Westport, CT: Praeger, 2007), pp. 36–37.
2. "The Shipman Inquiry: First Report," Dame Janet Smith, DBE, Chairman, July 2002, p. 187, http://murderpedia.org/male.S/images/shipman-harold/reports/first-report/first-report.pdf (accessed June 26, 2015).
3. *Indiana v. Orville Lynn Majors* Probable Cause Affidavit, http://murderpedia.org/male.M/m/majors-orville-affidavit.htm (accessed June 23, 2015).
4. Ibid.
5. Nick Schneider, "10 Years Ago: Linton Native Orville Lynn Majors Was Found Guilty of Six Murders and His Earliest Possible Release Date from Prison Is July 1, 2177," *Green County Daily World*, October 16, 2009, http://www.gcdailyworld.com/story/1579468.html (accessed June 24, 2015).
6. "Charles Edmund Cullen," *Murderpedia*, http://murderpedia.org/male.C/c/cullen-charles.htm (accessed June 26, 2015).
7. Harvey Rosenfeld, *Depravity: A Narrative of 16 Serial Killers* (iUniverse, 2009).
8. Colin Wilson and Donald Seaman, *The Serial Killers: A Study in the Psychology of Violence* (London, England: Virgin Books, 2007), p. 52.
9. Ibid., p. 53.
10. Robert M. Kaplan, *Medical Murder: Disturbing Cases of Doctors Who Kill* (Crows Nest, Australia: Allen & Unwin, 2009), p. 128.
11. Michael Newton, *The Encyclopedia of Serial Killers (Facts on File Crime Library)*, 2nd ed. (New York: Facts on File, 2006), p. 2.

12. Helen Birch, *Moving Targets: Women, Murder and Representation* (Berkeley, CA: University of California Press, 1994), p. 227.
13. Jennifer Furio, *Team Killers: A Comparative Study of Collaborative Criminals* (New York: Algora Publishing, 2001), p. 182.
14. Ramsland, p. 78.
15. Birch, p. 223.
16. Paul Lieberman, "Digging Deep for 'Angel's' Terrible Toll," *Los Angeles Times*, April 29, 2002, http://articles.latimes.com/2002/apr/29/news/mn-40609 (accessed June 30, 2015).
17. Paul Lieberman, "Graveyard Shift," *Los Angeles Times*, April 28, 2002, http://articles.latimes.com/2002/apr/28/news/mn-40474 (accessed June 30, 2015).
18. Paul Lieberman, "Digging Deep for 'Angel's' Terrible Toll," *Los Angeles Times*, April 29, 2002, http://articles.latimes.com/2002/apr/29/news/mn-40609 (accessed June 30, 2015).
19. "Efren Saldivar," *Murderpedia*, http://murderpedia.org/male.S/s/saldivar-efren.htm (accessed July 6, 2015).
20. Ramsland, p. 88.
21. R.J. Parker et al., *2015 Serial Killers True Crime Anthology, Volume II* (West Nyack, NY: Parker Publishing, Inc.), p. 194.
22. Ibid., p. 170.
23. Ibid., p. 172.

Chapter 2: The Comfort-Oriented Hedonists

1 . James Alan Fox and Jack Levin, *Extreme Killing: Understanding Serial and Mass Murder* (New York: SAGE Publications, 2014), p. 129.
2. Kenneth J. Gibson, *Killer Doctors: The Ultimate Betrayal of Trust* (Castle Douglas, Scotland: Neil Wilson Publishing, 2012), p. 113.
3. Erik Larson, *The Devil in the White City* (New York: Vintage Books, 2003), p. 109.
4. Joshua A. Perper and Stephen J. Cina, *When Doctors Kill: Who, Why, and How* (Dordrecht, Netherlands: Springer Science + Business Media, 2010), p. 28.
5. Diana Britt Franklin, "A Poison Mind," *Cincinnati Magazine,* October 2006, 133–135, 198–203.
6. Patricia A. Martinelli, *True Crime, Ohio: The State's Most Notorious Cases* (Mechanicsburg, PA: Stackpole Books, 2014), p. 20.
7. Evelyn Lauter, "The 'Blonde Borgia,'" *Cincinnati Magazine,* December 1989, 157.
8. Ibid.
9. Hannah Scott, "Cecile Bombeek." In *Women Criminals: An Encyclopedia of People and Issues* (Santa Barbara, CA: ABC-CLIO, 2011), pp. 321–323.

10. "The Nun's Story," *Time Magazine.* March 13, 1978, http://content.time.com/time/subscriber/article/0,33009,919411-1,00.html (accessed June 18, 2015).
11. Ibid.
12. Tony Rennell, "The Baby Butcher: One of Victorian Britain's Most Evil Murderers Exposed," *The Daily Mail,* September 28, 2007, http://www.dailymail.co.uk/femail/article-484575/The-baby-butcher-One-Victorian-Britains-evil-murderers-exposed.html (accessed July 20, 2015).
13. Ibid.
14. Ibid.
15. Ibid.
16. David King, *Death in the City of Light: The Serial Killer of Nazi-Occupied Paris* (New York: Crown/Archetype, 2011), p. 21.
17. Ibid., p. 363.
18. Ibid., p. 338.
19. Peter Elkind, "The Death Shift," *Texas Monthly,* August 1983, 106–113, 180–197.
20. Emily Webb, *Angels of Death: Disturbing Real-Life Cases of Nurses and Doctors Who Kill* (Scoresby, Australia: Five Mile Press, 2015), p. 66.
21. Katherine Ramsland, *Inside the Minds of Healthcare Serial Killers: Why They Kill* (Westport, CT: Praeger, 2007), p. 63.
22. Eric Schmitt, "Nurse Known as Dedicated Worker," *New York Times*, November 17, 1987, http://www.nytimes.com/1987/11/17/nyregion/nurse-known-as-dedicated-worker.html (accessed June 24, 2015).
23. Ramsland, p. 64.
24. Ibid., p. 47.

Chapter 3: The Lust- and Thrill-Oriented Hedonists

1. Ronald M. Holmes and Stephen T. Holmes, *Serial Murder* (New York: SAGE, 2009), p. 123.
2. Peter Vronsky, *Female Serial Killers: How and Why Women Become Monsters* (New York: Penguin, 2007), p. 132.
3. Harold Schechter, *Fatal: The Poisonous Life of a Female Serial Killer* (New York: Simon & Schuster, 2003), p. 73.
4. Ibid., p. 60.
5. Vronsky, p. 128.
6. Ibid., p. 130.
7. Lowell Cauffiel, *Forever and Five Days* (New York: Kensington Publishing Corporation, 1997), p. 445.
8. Carol Anne Davis, *Women Who Kill: Profiles of Female Serial Killers* (London, England: Allison & Busby, 2014), p. 148.

9. Ibid., pp. 148–149.
10. Robert M. Kaplan, *Medical Murder: Disturbing Cases of Doctors Who Kill* (Crows Nest, Australia: Allen & Unwin, 2009), p. 35.

Chapter 4: The Treatment Serial Killers

1. Robert M. Kaplan, *Medical Murder: Disturbing Cases of Doctors Who Kill* (Crows Nest, Australia: Allen & Unwin, 2009), p. 12.
2. Linda Burfield Hazzard, *Fasting for the Cure of Disease* (Seattle: Harrison Publishing, 1908), p. 22.
3. Gregg Olsen, *Starvation Heights: A True Story of Murder and Malice in the Woods of the Pacific Northwest* (New York: Crown/Archetype, 2005), pp. 194–195.
4. Katherine Ramsland. *Inside the Minds of Healthcare Serial Killers: Why They Kill* (Westport, CT: Praeger, 2007), p. 17.
5. Brian Bromberger and Janet Fife-Yeomans, *Deep Sleep: Harry Bailey and the Scandal of Chelmsford* (East Roseville, NSW, Australia: Simon & Schuster Australia, 1991), p. 2.
6. Kaplan, p. 157.
7. Ibid., p. 165.
8. Bromberger and Fife-Yeomans, pp. 5–6.
9. Kaplan, p. 147.
10. Marc Dewey, et al., "Ernst Ferdinand Sauerbruch and His Ambigious Role in the Period of National Socialism," *Annals of Surgery* 244, no. 2 (August 2006): 315–321, http://www.ncbi.nlm.nih.gov/pmc/articles/PMC1602148/ (accessed July 30, 2015).
11. "Ferdinand Sauerbruch (1875–1951)—Thoracic Surgeon," *Journal of the American Medical Association,* October 12, 1964, 152.
12. Kaplan, p. 148.
13. Ibid., p. 150.

Conclusion

1. Sarah Gregory et al., "Punishment and Psychopathy: A Case-Control Functional MRI Investigation of Reinforcement Learning in Violent Antisocial Personality Disordered Men," *The Lancet Psychiatry*, February 2015, 153–160.
2. Christopher Wanjek, "Psychopath's Brains Don't Grasp Punishment, Scans Reveal," *LiveScience,* January 28, 2015, http://www.livescience.com/49613-psychopaths-brains-punishment.html (accessed July 30, 2015).

Glossary

antisocial personality disorder (APD)—A condition characterized by continuous and chronic antisocial behavior in which the rights of others or generally accepted social norms are violated.

barbituate—A type of sedative drug that depresses the respiratory rate, temperature, and central nervous system; it is very addictive.

coma—A state of prolonged unconsciousness that can be caused by a variety of problems, including traumatic brain injury, stroke, or drug or alcohol intoxication; doctors will often intentionally induce comas to allow the brain to heal after a traumatic injury.

dementia—A progressive brain disorder caused by disease or injury, marked by memory loss, personality changes, and impaired reasoning.

depression—A mood disorder that causes a persistent feeling of sadness and loss of interest in day-to-day activities.

electroconvulsive therapy (ECT)—A way of treating mental illness by applying electric shocks to the brain.

intensive care unit (ICU)—A hospital ward containing special equipment and specially trained personnel to care for seriously ill patients; also called a critical care unit (CCU).

Munchausen Syndrome—A condition, often beginning in childhood, in which people pretend to be sick or injure themselves in order to gain attention and sympathy.

Munchausen Syndrome by Proxy—A condition in which people cause life-threatening symptoms in their victims in order to draw attention to themselves.

muscle relaxant—A drug that reduces muscle tone; often used during anesthesia and in intensive care and emergency procedures to produce temporary paralysis.

narcissistic personality disorder (NPD)—A mental disorder in which people have an inflated sense of their own importance, a deep need for admiration, and a lack of empathy for others.

opiate (narcotic) drugs—Medications that relieve pain by blocking the intensity to pain signals reaching the brain; they are very addictive.

Medical Serial Killers

psychopathy—A personality disorder characterized by antisocial behavior, lack of empathy and remorse, lack of inhibitions, and bold behavior; sometimes also referred to as "sociopathy."

psychosis—A mental illness characterized by radical changes in personality, impaired functioning, and a distorted or nonexistent sense of objective reality.

quack—A person who pretends to have medical skills.

respirator—A machine used to modify air breathed through it.

sadist—A person who enjoys inflicting pain on others or seeing other people hurt.

ventilator—A machine used to provide artificial respiration.

Further Reading

Books

Davis, Carol Anne. *Doctors Who Kill: Profiles of Lethal Medics.* London, England: Allison & Busby, 2011.

Fox, James Allen and Jack Levin. *Extreme Killing: Understanding Serial and Mass Murder.* New York: SAGE Publications, 2014.

Gibson, Kenneth J. *Killer Doctors: The Ultimate Betrayal of Trust.* Castle Douglas, Scotland: Neil Wilson Publishing, 2012.

Schechter, Harold. *The A to Z Encyclopedia of Serial Killers.* New York: Pocket Books, 2012.

Vronsky, Peter and Michael Newton, eds. *2015 Serial Killers True Crime Anthology: Volume 2 (Annual Serial Killers Anthology).* RJ Parker Publishing, 2014.

Websites

Crime Museum: Crime Library
www.crimemuseum.org/crime-library

FBI: Serial Murders
www.fbi.gov/stats-services/publications/serial-murder

Movies

Angel of Death: The Beverly Allitt Story (TV Movie), 2005.

Shipman (TV Movie). Directed by Roger Bamford, 2002

Index